# Unshakable
# Man

# Unshakable Man

## Ron Auch

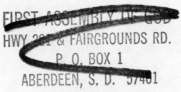

**New Leaf Press**

## Dedication

This book is dedicated to the two most influential men in my life. First of all, my dad. He is truly an "unshakable man" in his devotion to God. Secondly, to my father-in-law. His kind and gentle spirit is a true reflection of our Saviour.

## Acknowledgment

A simple thanks must go to John Cronce once again for his finishing touches on this manuscript. His faithfulness to God qualifies him to be an "unshakable man."

# Table of Contents:

# PART ONE

# Spiritual Leaders

# Chapter 1

# *Godly Leaders*

I had just finished eating breakfast at a favorite restaurant with a friend of mine when he said, "Have you ever considered why you were born in America?"

I looked at him a little puzzled and said, "Not really."

"Don't you find it interesting," he continued, "that you weren't born in some poverty stricken or godforsaken country where you would have no freedoms or possibility of bettering yourself?"

By now he had my attention, "That is an interesting thought!" I responded. "I guess it was a decision God made for me."

"That's it exactly," he said. "God chose this for us. We had no say in this decision at all, so He must have a reason for it." My friend didn't really have much more to say about this matter but it did cause some interesting thoughts.

Have you ever considered why you are a man? Did you choose your role in life? Did God give you the opportunity before you were born to decide whether you wanted to be a male or female? Obviously, none of us had a part in that decision. It was completely up to God.

We have been appointed to be what we are. Along with any appointment comes certain responsibilities. God has appointed men to be defenders. They are also leaders and providers. This is not to say that a woman could not function in any of these roles. Many women have been forced to become something they may not have chosen for themselves because of men failing to be what God wants them to be. What we are dealing with is the God-given roles He has appointed to each different sex. It's what the Bible calls nature.

The book of Isaiah shows us step by step what happens to a nation when men fail to function in their God-given roles. It ultimately leads to the destruction of its society. In Isaiah 1:4 we read, "Ah, sinful nation, a people loaded with guilt, a brood of evildoers, children given to corruption! They have forsaken the Lord; they have spurned the Holy One of Israel and turned their backs on him."

The prophet begins by describing the spiritual condition of Israel. He says, "They have forsaken the Lord." The key to turning any society back to God is through getting men to follow their God-given roles. We see this in the instruction Isaiah then gives to the men in verse 7: "Learn to do right! Seek justice, encourage the oppressed. Defend the cause of the fatherless, plead the case of the widow." When men function in the role to which God has appointed them, all goes well with the country. However, when men are disobedient to God, eventually God removes them from their appointed roles and puts individuals in places of leadership that cannot give proper guidance.

### Removal of the Supply and Support

Isaiah 3:1 gives us something important to consider:

"See now, the Lord, the Lord Almighty, is about to take from Jerusalem and Judah both supply and support: all supplies of food and all supplies of water." The prophet begins to describe what happens to a country that lacks godly men. First, God removes both supply and support. This deals with the natural food resources. The food sources dry up because the support system is gone. The support system for food is water. You can have wonderfully fertile soil, and you can have the most choice seed, but if there is no water, there is no growth. All of this is removed because the people of the land will not turn from their sin. The removal of these things are not meant so much to be punishment, but rather a desperate attempt on God's part to draw us back to Him.

I have had many opportunities to teach a Pastor's School in Uganda, Africa. This used to be one of the most beautiful countries of all Africa. People would travel from around the world to see the wild animals that roamed free there. Things are quite different in Uganda today. Currently it has the highest rate of AIDS (per capita) in the whole world. Hunger and starvation are quite common, all the water must be boiled before it can be drank because the food support systems have been removed from this country. How is it this once beautiful country has become what it is today?

The pastor I work with in Africa talked with me about when he was a little boy in Africa and his father, who pastored the church, would call the people to prayer. However, not many would respond. The pastor would warn the people over and over, "We must pray! If we don't, something terrible will happen to our country." Even with his desperate cries the people were not convinced that anything bad would happen to their beautiful country. One day it happened! On the television screen the regular programming was interrupted with this message, "The following churches have been officially closed by an order of the government." Their church was the first one on the list.

A dictator took over the government and began to wreak havoc throughout the country. He would purposely send his soldiers into the jungle to target practice on the wild animals. He chopped down the trees for no reason at all. By the time he was forced out of office he had completely devastated the country. Before the takeover of this cruel taskmaster people were quite inattentive to their spiritual need. The pastor could hardly get them to respond to any spiritual pursuits. Today it is quite different. Christianity is growing at a rapid rate. The country is recovering nicely. Godly men are at the helm once again. If men will not seek God in the good times, God knows exactly what they need to go through to bring them back to Him.

### Removal of the Leaders

"The hero and warrior, the judge and prophet, the soothsayer and elder, the captain of fifty and man of rank, the counselor, skilled craftsman and clever enchanter" (Isa. 3:2-3). These two verses continue to describe that which God is removing from the country. These are all the natural leaders of the country. There will be no more heroes. The judges of the land will lack integrity. The "prophets" will speak "words" to those who have itching ears instead of speaking the true Word of God. The captain of 50 represents the type of man we refer to as "a leader of leaders." When all these leaders are removed, the society crumbles.

### Inexperienced Leaders

"I will make boys their officials; mere children will govern them" (Isa. 3:4). Immature individuals will become leaders. Obviously, this can be a reference to young people gaining positions of leadership, but a person can be chronologically old and yet immature. Contextually, good leadership is defined as someone who follows God and is obedient to Him. "Mere children as leaders," could simply be those who refuse to submit themselves to God. They lack spiritual maturity. Subsequently they know very little of what true leadership is.

A leader must first be led. Spiritually speaking, a man cannot lead others unless he follows God. All spiritual leadership comes from the Lord. If a man will submit to God, God can lead him. As he is being led, he can lead others. Without that, he will remain immature in true spiritual leadership skills. Sometimes when you challenge men to become better spiritual leaders, their first inclination is to become more domineering and demanding.

Spiritual leadership differs from what the world calls leadership. A spiritual leader must first be led by God. This calls for submission on his part. Submission develops into humility which ultimately exemplifies the character of Christ. To lead spiritually, you do not do much more than direct others toward Christ through your own pursuit of Christ. The apostle Paul was a great example of this. In Philippians 4:9 we read, "Whatever you have learned or received or heard from me, or seen in me — put it into practice. And the God of peace will be with you."

Isaiah 3:5 goes on to say: "People will oppress each other — man against man, neighbor against neighbor. The young will rise up against the old, the base against the honorable."

"People will oppress each other," means society will lose that "friendly neighborhood" feeling. "Neighbor against neighbor" can mean that suing your neighbor will come into vogue. "The young will rise up against the old, the base against the honorable" means society will have lost all reverence for the elderly. The phrase "Respect your elders" will be mocked amongst the young.

### No Leadership Available

"A man will seize one of his brothers at his father's home, and say, "You have a cloak, you be our leader; take charge of this heap of ruins!" (Isa. 3:6). We will search for leadership, but it will be hard to find. "You have a cloak, you be our leader" means material wealth will become the criteria for leadership. America has made materialism its God for so long that we, too, are looking to those who are "materially successful" as the only ones qualified to lead.

"But in that day he will cry out, 'I have no remedy. I have no food or clothing in my house; do not make me the leader of the people' " (Isa. 3:7). No one wants to take responsibility. A brother will turn down his own brother because he doesn't want to take charge of this "heap of ruins." Do you understand what's missing here? True godly leadership! A good leader will take a ruin and turn it around. That's what leadership is all about. However, God has removed the leaders, and subsequently those who are left to lead don't know how to handle the responsibility.

Today the Church is suffering from the lack of godly leadership. It is getting harder and harder for pastors to find men, first of all that qualify to be deacons, and secondly, want to lead.

### Homosexuality

Let's continue to consider what happens to a society when men fail to be leaders, both spiritually and naturally. "The look on their faces testifies against them; they parade their sin like Sodom; they do not hide it. Woe to them! They have brought disaster upon themselves" (Isa. 3:9). When men fail to live in submission to God, they eventually give themselves over to unnatural affections. The Bible tells us that this typically ends up in a homosexual movement. Paul, the Apostle, knew this, also. In Romans 1:20-21 he states, "For since the creation of the world God's invisible qualities — his eternal power and divine nature — have been clearly seen, being understood from what has been made, so that men are without excuse. For although they knew God, they neither glorified him as God nor gave thanks to him, but their thinking became futile and their foolish hearts were darkened."

Isaiah and Paul are teaching us that the most natural state for a man is to be dependent upon God. When men live independently from God they are in an unnatural state of being. This is reflected in society by men loving men, women loving women, and children becoming leaders. Consider Paul's words: "Because of this, God gave them over to shameful lusts. Even their women exchanged natural relations for unnatural ones. In the same way the men also abandoned natural relations with women and were inflamed with lust for one another. Men committed indecent acts with other men, and received in themselves the due penalty for their perversion. Furthermore, since they did not think it worthwhile to retain the knowledge of God, he gave them over to a depraved mind, to do what ought not to be done. They have become filled with every kind of wickedness, evil, greed and depravity. They are full of envy, murder, strife, deceit and malice. They are gossips, slanderers, God-haters, insolent, arrogant and boastful; they invent ways of doing evil; they disobey their parents; they are senseless, faithless, heartless, ruthless. Although they know God's righteous decree that those who do such things deserve death, they not only continue to do these very things but also approve of those who practice them" (Rom. 1:26-32).

Homosexuality is not the true problem being addressed in these verses. The true problem is independence from God. Independence from God is an unnatural state for man to live in. When he lives in an unnatural state, that which was natural becomes unnatural. The same can be said of the Church. Prayerlessness indicates independence from God. When the Church is prayerless many things that were once called sin are no longer considered off-limits at all. Today the Church participates in many things that the former Church would never have even talked about. The Church is just as wrong in justifying its worldliness as the homosexual is in defending his attraction to the same sex.

## God's Nature

God has made His nature very clear to us. Paul says that the way God has revealed His nature is from "what has been made, so that men are without excuse." Since we are created in His image, His nature is not a difficult thing for us to grasp. There is a naturalness that comes to both women and men. However, if we fail to glorify God our thinking becomes futile and our hearts are darkened. The result of that is unnatural affections.

Isaiah says, "They parade their sin like Sodom; they do not hide it. Woe to them! They have brought disaster upon themselves" (Isa. 3:9). They have become proud of their sin. They have come out of the closet and have attempted to gain some level of respect in society. The problem with the idea of accepting them as normal means that the normal nature of a man has been altered. This goes completely contrary to what God says in His Word.

## Women Leaders

When men become effeminate, women take up the leadership of the country, hence a women's movement. With women taking positions of leadership, we have a complete reversal of natural roles. Society then becomes quite twisted. "Youths oppress my people, women rule over them. O my people, your guides lead you astray; they turn you from the path" (Isa. 3:12). "Your guides lead you astray." This is referring to the leadership of the women. This does not mean that women do not have the capability of leading, this is dealing with the unnaturalness of this particular situation. The reason the women are leading is because men have failed in their responsibilities of leadership. It's not that women can't lead, it's that God has designed the man to be a leader and when he fails, then those who replace him are misled in their leadership.

Consider this: Men lead from a position of risk and faith, while women lead from a position of safety and security. Because men are providers by nature, they tend to lead from that perspective. Men are somewhat predisposed to taking a more relaxed outlook in leadership matters because they have an inner sense of being able to come up with whatever they will need for whatever situation may come up. They may not really be able to supply whatever they need, however, that tends to be their approach.

Women differ by nature in leadership. God has created the woman with a need for security and she regularly leads from that perspective. What we are dealing with here are tendencies, not inevitabilities. It certainly is possible to find both men and women that are exceptions in their leadership styles.

The difference in leadership styles is reflected in how men and women mature. It is very typical for a young girl to mature much quicker than a young boy. The average male sees maturity as something he will work at when he needs to, whereas the average female sees maturity as something she needs to achieve. The male leads from a similar perspective. When the time comes he will do whatever he needs to do. The female leads from a different perspective. Her outlook comes from her need for security, subsequently she prepares much sooner.

Men lead from a faith perspective that says, "Whatever we need will be there when we need it." Women lead from a security perspective that says, "Everything must be in place in case we need it."

## The Need for Security

Typically a woman gains security from her husband's relationship with God. If she is married to a man who does not seek God, she tends to be insecure. From her insecurity, she then tries to control her world. This is why women focus more on social issues when they are in positions of authority than men do. We often see this in government. When there is an effeminate influence in government, welfare concerns often take precedent over the security of the nation, at least in regards to the military. This may make the woman sound weak, but actually she isn't. She simply has a different natural role.

A woman's need for security can actually work to her advantage IF her husband loves her the way Christ loves the Church. "Husbands, love your wives, just as Christ loved the church and gave himself up for her" (Eph. 5:25). If a man actually loves his wife the way he is supposed to, then his wife's needs will drive him to a deeper pursuit of God. If he understands that her security comes from his relationship with God, that will continually push him toward God. It's a wonderful plan, but the qualifier is that a man love his wife the way Christ loves the Church. Here again is where the plan falls short if the man is not godly. Everything comes down to leadership. I know a pastor who continually pumps that thought into younger ministers. He often says, "Every problem is a problem with leadership."

## Grace Versus Law

Consider what has happened to our society since women have become leaders. "Your guides lead you astray" (Isa. 3:12). Naturally speaking, women represent grace while men represent the law. Grace covers sin, the law reveals sin. "When the woman saw that the fruit of the tree was good for food and pleasing to the eye, and also desirable for gaining wisdom, she took some and ate it. She also gave some to her husband, who was with her, and he ate it" (Gen. 3:6). Eve ate the fruit and thought nothing of it. Then she gave some to her husband, and he ate it, also. Consider what happened after Adam ate the fruit. "Then the eyes of both of them were opened, and they realized that they were naked; so they sewed fig leaves together and made coverings for themselves" (Gen. 3:7). "Then the eyes of both of them were opened." Eve represents grace. Grace covers sin. Grace does not see wrongdoing. Adam represents the law. The law reveals sin. It was not until Adam ate of the fruit that their eyes were opened and they saw that what they did was wrong.

## Different Perspectives

Typically men and women differ drastically in how they see things. One day when my son was quite young, he built a ramp for his bicycle. He set it up on the sidewalk and then would peddle his bicycle as hard as he could and then jump his bike off it. He did not build it very strong and by about the third time when his front wheel hit the ramp it fell over, and he crashed. He went head over heels. It was not very serious. He did hurt his elbow — but mostly his pride.

Later that same day, my wife and I were driving in our car with our son in the back seat. He was still licking his wounds and whimpering a little bit when his mom turned to him and said, "Oh, I wish I was hurting instead of you." When she said that, I sat there amazed because at the exact same time I was thinking to myself, *It's good for him to be hurting like this.* Both positions are compassionate. They are simply displayed differently. Mom wanted to take the hurt herself — that's grace speaking. Dad felt his son needed to reap what he sowed in order to keep him from doing it again — that's the law speaking.

Our children need the balance of both grace and the law. They need both mom and dad. When one is missing, there tends to be an overbalance on one side. In America, for the most part, men have abandoned their homes. They have abandoned their responsibilities. Subsequently, moms are raising the majority of the children. Mom is fully capable. This is not a discussion of her abilities. This is a discussion of the natural roles both men and women have. Moms are doing the best they can, but without dad there is a problem. Mom represents grace. An all-grace perspective will corrupt, whereas an all-law perspective will crush. Our kids would be no better off being raised by dad only. That would be like being raised in a military academy.

### Political Correctness

Obviously I am dealing with this issue from a general sense. You can find exceptions to anything. There are moms who have abandoned their children, but for the most part it's dad that has left home. In large measure, mom has been left alone. That has resulted in what we call a politically correct society. Political correctness, which never deals with anything harshly, is the corruption that has come from an all-grace upbringing. I remember when a young American man was going to get spanked with a cane (whipped) in Singapore. While visiting that country, he went on a senseless spree of vandalism, seriously damaging nearly a dozen cars. The legal punishment for such a crime in Singapore was caning. The national news media thought this was just terrible. They said that this was one of the worst things that could ever happen. It became an international incident.

An all-grace perspective wants to cover sin. This has resulted in hardly even punishing criminals, giving animals the same rights as humans, and making it criminal to say insensitive words to another person. Most of these things would never have developed into such extremes in our society if men had maintained their role.

After the prophet Isaiah says that our leaders lead us astray, he says, "They turn you from the path" (Isa. 3:12). God sets every nation on a path toward righteousness. As long as that nation lives in obedience to God, they stay on that particular path. Those who take over when men fail to lead turn us from the path that God would have us on. Those most responsible to keep a nation on the path of righteousness are the ministers. Earlier in Isaiah 3:2 we read, "The hero and warrior, the judge and prophet, the soothsayer and elder." This is part of the list of godly leaders that God removed from the nation. One of those leaders is the prophet. This does not mean there will be no prophets. It simply means that most of the prophets will not speak the true Word of God. You will be hard pressed to find true men of God.

This is another result of the all-grace society we have developed. Many young men who have been raised from this perspective have gone into the ministry. The way this manifests itself is through the sinless message they preach. They find it too harsh to preach against sin. Preaching against sin is not politically correct. It is being too insensitive to those who are sinning. They preach a message of love, joy, and peace. Certainly that is part of the gospel. Jesus is the Prince of Peace. God is love. However, God is also holy and if we don't preach the balance we will distort the true image of God.

Consider the Word of God concerning these "priests and prophets:" "From the least to the greatest, all are greedy for gain; prophets and priests alike, all practice deceit. They dress the wound of my people as though it were not serious. 'Peace, peace,' they say, when there is no peace" (Jer. 6:13-14).

Whatever happened to men of God who could stand before the people of God and declare the error of their ways? I'm afraid they left with the dads. We need men of God who live in the fear of God rather than the fear of man — men who denounce the worldliness in the Church and the corruption in the Christian home. We need men who can put us back on the path God has designed for us. Our current guides, the women and children, lead us astray.

### Judgment!

Consider God's remedy for the situation, "I will turn my hand against you; I will thoroughly purge away your dross and remove all your impurities" (Isa. 1:25). All is not lost. God has an answer. The answer is judgment! The problem in our society is that we have become filled with dross. The word "dross" means impurities. The impurities in this case come in the form of disobedience.

God will turn His hand against us. This represents a pressure in our lives. Pressure generally leads men to repentance. Repentance restores our relationship with God. It removes the dross from our lives. It leaves us with pure hearts. God is desirous to judge His people because He wants to reconcile His people to Him. In that light, judgment is an act of mercy. God will have mercy on any repentant heart. If you are not the man of God you need to be, bring your life back into obedience to God.

Through repentance, God will restore leaders to society. "I will restore your judges as in days of old, your counselors as at the beginning" (Isa. 1:26). There is hope for the nation, but it lies within the hearts of godly men. If the world ever needed men who know God, it's today. We struggle, not only as a nation, but our whole world is feeling the effects of men having abandoned their obedience to God. This book is a desperate call for men to be men, and specifically, godly men. However, the solution is not in just being a man, it's in being a man who follows after God. The last thing this book needs to be is an exaltation of maleness. God is the only hope, and Jesus is the only way to God. When men follow God, all others follow along.

# Chapter 2

# *Violent Men*

If men are going to be the kind of spiritual leaders they need to be, they will need to know how to handle the attacks of the enemy. I once heard a great Christian leader say, "How can we hope to come into spiritual battle?" At first I thought his comments were a little off-base. Why would we *want* to come into spiritual battle? Then he concluded his thoughts by saying in essence, "The only people who are involved with spiritual battle are those who are doing something for God. Those who are not doing anything for the Lord are the ones who pose no threat to the enemy."

"And from the days of John the Baptist until now the kingdom of heaven suffereth violence, and the violent take it by force" (Matt. 11:12; KJV). In referring to the kingdom of heaven suffering violence, we often think in terms of Satan actually bringing violence into God's realm. That would be a misapplication of this verse. This is actually referring to the fact that God's kingdom forcefully advances. In other words, anything that gains heaven does so through a struggle. There is a battle that is waged over the soul of every man. Spiritual warfare is a struggle over the soul of man. Both God and Satan have the same objectives in this battle. Because of the opposition there is to a man surrendering his life to Christ, God is looking for violent men who know how to take heaven by force, to join with Him in this struggle over a man's soul. God is looking for those who will enter into this arena and never give up until there is victory.

We need to understand what it is to be one of the violent men referred to in this verse and also what it actually is to take heaven by force. First, the violent man. The word "violence" in this verse does not mean what we typically think of when we hear this word. We often associate violence with crime or harming another person. However, in this verse the word simply means "impetuous, unrelenting, or forceful." The violent men who take heaven by force are unrelenting, forceful men. We are to be as unrelenting in our opposition of Satan as he is to us Christians.

My home is close to Lake Michigan. Periodically I go for a walk on an exercise path along the lake. I have noticed that each time I walk along the lake, its waters are lapping up against the shoreline. Sometimes it's quite calm, other times it's turbulent, depending on the weather. Regardless of whether it's calm or turbulent, it is always wearing away the shoreline. This not only paints a picture of how Satan constantly wears away at the saints, but also how we are to constantly oppose him. We must be as unrelenting against the enemy as he is against us.

### Take It By Force

We have developed a rather physical perspective on "taking heaven by force." You do not need to be a hunk of a man with bulging biceps in order to "take it by force." In spiritual warfare, we are dealing with spiritual force, which differs greatly from physical force. Ephesians 6:10 sums this up quite nicely: "Finally, be strong in the Lord and in his mighty power." That is our objective, we want to become strong in God. How is that accomplished? Spiritually speaking, how do we develop strength? Interestingly enough, spiritual strength is born out of rest; specifically, rest in the Lord. Our spiritual strength is born out of our time in the presence of the Lord.

Isaiah 40:31 says, "But those who hope in the Lord will renew their strength. They will soar on wings like eagles; they will run and not grow weary, they will walk and not be faint." The word "hope" in this verse means "to tarry or wait." It also means to be braided. In other words, those who are braided to the Lord, those who have developed a deep attachment to Him, find that when He soars like an eagle, they do also. However, they simply ride on His strength. When one is attached to God in this manner, he finds that he can run and not grow weary, or he can walk and not faint because he is simply riding on the strength of his relationship with God. This illustrates how our spiritual strength is born out of our rest in the Lord.

There is a big difference between how spiritual strength is developed and how physical strength is developed. This is what confuses us in our physical world. Spiritual strength comes through resting in the Lord, whereas physical strength comes through exertion. Physical strength develops through pitting yourself against something else. In spiritual warfare, we are not to pit ourselves against anything even though we are called to be unrelenting in our opposition of Satan. What we tend to forget is that the battle is the Lord's. We are to simply attach ourselves to Him and walk with Him through this fight. It is His battle and the way we engage in it is through developing a deep, intimate relationship with God. When we lose sight of that important fact we tend to look at spiritual battle through the eyes of the flesh. We study the enemy for all he's worth. We develop strategies and make all sorts of plans. I contend that Satan has side-tracked the Church into fighting him rather than pursuing Christ. We have lost sight of the biblical fact that our pursuit of Christ is the very thing that renders the enemy powerless.

There is an old illustration that still makes an important point today. When the FBI trains someone to identify counterfeit money they do so by having them study real money, not counterfeit money. Counterfeit money can change a thousand ways. There is too much to know about it. All you really need to know is what's real — then anything that is not real becomes quite obvious. The same is true spiritually. We do not need to study the enemy as much as we need to study and know Christ. If we know Jesus, then anything that is not Jesus becomes quite obvious. The enemy is the father of lies, he can appear a thousand different ways. He can even appear as an angel of light. We don't need to know nearly as much about him as we do Jesus.

### Consistency

The strength for everything, whether physical or spiritual, comes through consistency. Consistency in physical exercise develops physical strength. Consistency in spiritual activities develops spiritual strength. We cannot think of spiritual strength as a muscle, the way we think of physical strength. Spiritual strength is godly character. How could a person be considered spiritual without emulating the Lord? Character, therefore, becomes our greatest asset in spiritual battle. Without consistency in our pursuit of God, we fail to develop in His character. It is from the great lack of godly character in the Church today that we feel the enemy is trampling us. "You are the salt of the earth. But if the salt loses its saltiness, how can it be made salty again? It is no longer good for anything, except to be thrown out and trampled by men" (Matt. 5:13). When the salt loses its saltiness, it no longer possesses the ability to create thirst. When people no longer thirst for what we have, they will trample us. The solution to our problem is not to mount a great offensive front. The solution is to go back to seeking God consistently. Without a real change of character, the Church cannot hope to gain much ground spiritually. The character of God is the saltiness that must be restored to the Church.

Consistency in our pursuit is what develops God's character within us. Consistency denotes denial. In order to be consistent, one must continually deny himself. It takes self-denial to pray with real consistency. It's takes self-denial to read the Bible consistently. When you deny self, you take on God's character. Most of what we call spiritual battle today is nothing more than the problems we are running into because of our lack of character. This is not to say that there isn't any demonic activity; there is. The Bible makes that very clear. From our lack of understanding the difference between demonic activity and flesh problems, we have become more anxious than we need to be.

### Spiritual Defense

I once heard the late Rev. Donald Barnhouse explain this dilemma on a cassette tape, in a message he preached in 1957. I will paraphrase it for you here.

Our military understands that you need to identify your source of attack before you can properly defend yourself. Suppose an office building, situated on the ocean front, was destroyed by a bomb. The FBI rushes to the scene to begin their investigation. As they are going about their task someone comes up to the captain and asks what he is doing. "I am securing this area so we can catch the terrorist that blew up this building," he replies.

"This won't do you any good because it wasn't a terrorist that blew up this building, it was a submarine. An enemy submarine got close enough to shoot up a missile and that's what blew up the building."

"Well then," the captain said, "if it was a submarine we need to get the navy."

The navy is alerted and the admiral is getting his troops ready to go after the enemy sub. As they are preparing someone comes up to the admiral and says, "What are you doing?"

"We are going after the submarine that blew up this building," he said.

"Well this won't do you any good because the building didn't blow up because of a submarine, it was an airplane. An enemy airplane came by and dropped a bomb and that's what blew up the building."

The admiral replied, "Then we must alert the air force."

This is a very simple illustration but it makes a very important point. Our military knows that you don't use a high-speed jet to go down a back alley to catch a terrorist. You don't use a submarine to go after a high-speed jet. You also don't use the FBI in their cars to go after a submarine. If you don't know how you are being attacked you don't know how to defend yourself.

The Scripture indicates that we struggle with three basic things: the world, the devil, and the flesh. These are our three problem areas. One of the problems we are facing is that we are trying to apply deliverance to every problem we have. Deliverance applies to satanic problems only. Deliverance does not apply to flesh or worldly problems.

## The World, the Devil, the Flesh

A lady once came up to Dr. Barnhouse and said, "Pastor, I need to tell you about a certain couple in our church. They are the most worldly people I know."

Barnhouse said, "I know this couple. I don't know them to be that worldly."

"Pastor," she said, "they smoke cigarettes."

"Smoking cigarettes is not worldly. That's a flesh problem," he said.

"Well pastor, they are social drinkers," she responded.

"Social drinking is not as much worldly as it is a weakness of the flesh also," he said. Barnhouse then looked at the woman and said, "From all I can see, you may very well be the most worldly person in the whole church."

She was quite taken back at that and said, "But pastor, I don't smoke or drink."

"I didn't say you did. I said you were worldly," he replied.

Barnhouse went on to explain that worldliness finds its root in pride. Pride is the exaltation of self. It's because we want to be exalted in the eyes of men that things like fashion mean anything to us. It's because of pride that we involve ourselves in things like gossip. Gossip puts others down, thus it exalts the gossiper. Deliverance does not apply to worldliness. The Bible teaches us that the only way to overcome pride is to humble ourselves. "Humble yourselves before the Lord, and he will lift you up" (James 4:10). Humbling is something we are instructed to do. I cannot be prayed for to receive humility, because humility is a character trait which must be developed. Character is developed through denial of self. Second Chronicles 7:14 says, "If my people, who are called by my name, will humble themselves and pray and seek my face and turn from their wicked ways, then will I hear from heaven and will forgive their sin and will heal their land." The most we can do is to ask God for strength. Do you remember how strength comes? It comes through spending time in His presence. There is a big difference between developing strength of character and being delivered from something.

Deliverance does not apply to flesh problems, either. A person cannot be delivered from his flesh. The only people delivered from their flesh are those who are lying six feet under the ground. They have finally been set free. If you are alive, you cannot be set free from yourself. The Bible teaches us that we have to crucify the flesh — we are to flee from youthful lusts. Consider the following verse: "Put to death, therefore, whatever belongs to your earthly nature: sexual immorality, impurity, lust, evil desires and greed, which is idolatry" (Col. 3:5). We are instructed to "put to death" or "mortify" our fleshly nature. Again, this is something we must do; deliverance does not apply.

If you give yourself over to a flesh problem long enough, with no restraints, it may develop into a stronghold of the enemy. You may come to the place where you need someone to pray a prayer of deliverance for you. However, you must understand that all prayer will do is break Satan's grip in that area. After the prayer, you must still mortify your flesh. The Church today is making the mistake of applying deliverance to all things. What seems to be happening is that those who need to exercise self-discipline to their dilemma are seeking deliverance. A few days after they have been prayed for, the same old problem seems to surface again. This has led the Church into a discussion of whether or not a Christian can be demon possessed. Much of what we are calling spiritual battle today is really a struggle between the fleshly nature and God's nature.

### The Easy Yoke

"For my yoke is easy and my burden is light" (Matt.

11:30). How could a yoke ever be light? Only through consistency! Consistency builds strength. When I was in school, I was not a very good student. I didn't have real good study habits. Many times my report card would be sent home with a little message written on the bottom of it by my teacher. The message would say something like "Ron could do better if he would just try." Knowing that I could do it always satisfied me. I didn't think I needed to prove to the teachers what they seemed to know about me already. That was not the healthiest approach. I never did develop good study habits. My best friend, however, did. I can't even remember how many times the night before a test, I had to set aside the entire night to do in one night what I could have spread out over a period of several nights. I had to spend the whole night studying. The test threw my life into turmoil because I lacked consistency in my study habits. My friend, on the other hand, had excellent study habits. He would study a little each night. Therefore, the night before the test he simply did a little more than what he normally did. There was no panic in his life over an upcoming test. There was a calm assurance. Many times we would be walking to school and I would be praying that God would put something in my mind that I hadn't put there. All the while my buddy walked along in peace. Consistency had given him a strength to draw from.

One day I received a phone call from my mother. She had found my father passed out on the bathroom floor suffering from a bleeding ulcer. There was blood all over. The paramedics came and said they could not find a pulse. It was a very serious matter. She called to ask me to pray. I did pray. I even prayed more than I normally prayed, but I also had a simple assurance that once I had prayed there was nothing more for me to do, for it was in God's hands. I didn't even feel the need to worry. Others criticized me for not seeming to care about my father, because I didn't act worried about him. It wasn't that I didn't care, it's that I had a strength to draw from so that it was not necessary to go into a panic.

I believe the consistency of my prayer life, which includes praying for my family, is a testimony of caring. Since I had the habit of praying for them on a consistent basis, on the day of trial there was no need to panic. There is, however, an honest sense that God is more concerned for their welfare than I am. I can rest in that.

If a person exercised physically everyday, he would build up a source of strength. He may not need to use his strength to its full extent everyday. However, if he will exercise everyday, he will have a storehouse to draw from on the day that his strength is needed. The storehouse of strength is called consistency.

"Come to me, all you who are weary and burdened, and I will give you rest" (Matt. 11:28). In this verse Jesus is calling us to himself. "Come to me." That's the call to intimacy. Through intimacy with God, we come into a resting place. Spiritual strength is born out of our rest in God.

"Take my yoke upon you and learn from me, for I am gentle and humble in heart, and you will find rest for your souls" (Matt. 11:29). Here Jesus tells us to learn from Him, He is gentle and humble. This is very interesting; earlier in this same chapter Jesus calls for violent, unrelenting, forceful men. Now He says, "Learn from me, for I am gentle and humble." There seems to be a conflict here. How could violent, unrelenting men be humble and gentle also? It's really very simple. This is spiritual, not physical.

Jesus is teaching us that we are up against a most powerful foe. We are no match for Satan in our own strength. Our only strength against the enemy lies in the character of Christ. If we approach Satan in our own strength he will simply say, "Jesus I know, and I know about Paul, but who are you?" (Acts 19:15). Do you understand? There is no physical application to a spiritual situation. The violent, forceful, unrelenting men who know how to take it by force are simply those who emulate the character of Jesus. Those who walk as Jesus walked are the most powerful men on earth.

## Pride Versus Humility

I want to refer to Rev. Donald Barnhouse again in an illustration I heard him once give. He was challenging his listeners to consider what was really going on when Satan tempted Jesus in the wilderness. In this struggle, you have the pinnacle of pride versus the pinnacle of humility. Satan is pride. Because of his pride, he lost his place in heaven. Jesus is humility. He came to this earth born in a manger. Amongst men, He had no ranking. Barnhouse believed that Satan was having a problem with Jesus beating him as a man and not as God. Pride never wants to be defeated, especially by something it considers less than self. It seems Satan was saying in essence, "If You are going to beat me, beat me as God, not as a man."

It is one thing to be beaten by a champion. It is another thing to be beaten by a wimp. If you got into a boxing match with the world's heavyweight champion, and at one point he hit you in the eye and gave you a black eye, that would not be such a disgrace. You could say to others, "The world's heavyweight champion did this to me." However, if you got into a boxing match with someone much smaller than yourself and he also gave you a black eye, that is probably not something you would feel led to share with anyone.

"The tempter came to him and said, 'If you are the Son of God, tell these stones to become bread' " (Matt.

4:3). When Satan said this, he was in essence saying, "Use Your power. Beat me as God, not as a man." Look at how Jesus responded to him: "It is written: 'Man does not live on bread alone, but on every word that comes from the mouth of God' " (Matt. 4:4). Jesus said "Man." Jesus was beating Satan as a man. His character was defeating him. This is why Satan will fight your personal prayer life more than anything else. He knows that through giving yourself to God in prayer, His character develops in you. He does not want you to develop the same character that beat him in the wilderness.

Satan is never defeated by going head to head against him. He is defeated by becoming the opposite of him. You cannot defeat pride in another person's life by becoming more proud than they are. Pride is defeated by humility. Demonic encounter is not a power encounter, it is a truth encounter. The truth sets us free because it is the opposite of the father of lies. We are to put on the garment of praise to be set free from the spirit of heaviness.

Certainly there is demonic activity in the heavenlies. We have biblical accounts of angels fighting with demons. However, spiritual battle takes place on a one-on-one plain, also. Spiritual battle can come in the form of temptation. If you are being tempted and you could give into that thing and no one in the world would ever find out, it will take the character of Christ to pull you through.

Jesus says, "Take my yoke upon you" (Matt. 11:29). A salesman was once driving down a country road when he saw a farmer working his field. He was using two oxen. They were wearing the traditional yoke, but one of the animals was full-grown while the other was very young and much smaller. The salesman thought it was odd for the farmer to match these two animals up. He pulled his car over and went up to the farmer. He said,

"Why would you match these two animals together? Isn't it terribly hard for the smaller one to keep up with the larger one?"

The farmer responded, "I'll tell you what we are doing. We are teaching the young one how to plow." Then he said, "We have yoked him up to the larger more mature ox so he can learn his footsteps." Finally he said, "Because of the size of the larger animal, he is the one carrying all of the work load. The young one feels none of the work load, he is simply learning the footsteps of the older one."

Jesus says in essence, "Yoke yourself to Me!" What could we do to help Jesus? Once we are yoked to Him, do we say, "Okay, You can back off now, Jesus, I'll handle it from here." NO! Jesus carries the work load. The battle is the Lord's. We simply learn how to walk as He walks. Taking it by force is walking as Jesus walked. It's talking as Jesus talked. It's praying as Jesus prayed. It's following our Heavenly Father as Jesus followed His Heavenly Father.

# Chapter 3

# God's Warrior

What is it to be a soldier for the Lord? We need to consider a number of verses to gain a better understanding of this. In 2 Timothy 2:4-5 we read, "No one serving as a soldier gets involved in civilian affairs — he wants to please his commanding officer. Similarly, if anyone competes as an athlete, he does not receive the victor's crown unless he competes according to the rules."

Within Christendom there is a major call for spiritual men to engage in spiritual battle. For the most part there is nothing wrong with standing in opposition to the enemy. It seems, however, we have forgotten about something that is actually quite major. Our military would never send a man into battle without first having trained him. Our current fascination with spiritual battle lacks a focus on the condition of the warrior. It presumes that all those wanting to involve themselves in this endeavor are ready for battle. We need to take a serious look into the preparation of the warrior.

There is nothing broad about the kingdom of God. By that I mean not all those who make a profession of faith qualify. Consider the following verses. Matthew

7:13-14 says, "Enter through the narrow gate. For wide is the gate and broad is the road that leads to destruction, and many enter through it. But small is the gate and narrow the road that leads to life, and only a few find it." Luke 14:25-27 says, "Large crowds were traveling with Jesus, and turning to them he said: 'If anyone comes to me and does not hate his father and mother, his wife and children, his brothers and sisters — yes, even his own life — he cannot be my disciple. And anyone who does not carry his cross and follow me cannot be my disciple.' "

These verses indicate that the only way we can really be a good soldier is through a complete denial of self. Salvation is by grace. Grace cannot be earned. However, the Bible indicates that if you have sincerely given your life to Christ, then you will no longer live a self-centered existence. Jesus must occupy our entire being in order for us to gain the fullness of His life. The whole thought here is that the greatest indicator of your salvation is whether or not you are willing to walk the straight and narrow path.

It seems that churchgoers today believe they are Christians because of what they say about themselves. They call themselves Christians; therefore, they believe they are. Whether or not a person is a Christian is not determined by how he feels about himself, but rather by how the Word of God defines a Christian. We are not Christians because of what we say about Jesus, but because of what Jesus says about us.

Consider Matthew 7:21-23: "Not everyone who says to me, 'Lord, Lord,' will enter the kingdom of heaven, but only he who does the will of my Father who is in heaven. Many will say to me on that day, 'Lord, Lord, did we not prophesy in your name, and in your name drive out demons and perform many miracles?' Then I will tell them plainly, 'I never knew you. Away from me, you evildoers!' " In these verses, the people referred to themselves as Christians, they even called Jesus, "Lord." However, their own statements about themselves meant nothing. The only thing that meant anything was what Jesus said about them. Jesus said, "I never knew you."

In Mark 8:38 we read, "If anyone is ashamed of me and my words in this adulterous and sinful generation, the Son of Man will be ashamed of him when he comes in his Father's glory with the holy angels." What is it to be ashamed of Christ? It is to choose the wide path rather than the narrow path. The narrow path represents death to self. It means living entirely for Christ. The wide path represents self-centeredness. It means worldliness.

Many Christians have heaven as their only goal. The only thing they live for is going to heaven someday. Heaven is not to be our goal because heaven is automatic. If you are a Christian, you do not need to pursue that which will be the ultimate end of your life. The problem this creates is that if the only thing you are concerned with is going to heaven, then you tend to only do those things that you think will get you there. That develops into a self-centered motive.

Serving God is to be our goal, not just going to heaven one day. The reward for serving God will be heaven. However, living to serve God keeps you from becoming self-centered. You then base your activities on those things that will enhance your relationship with Jesus, not just those things that keep it in existence. I don't believe any Christian should be content with just being saved. We should be obsessed with living for God so that others can see Him through us.

When Christ returns, will He find you working for Him or just waiting to go to heaven? Working for Jesus is choosing the narrow path because of the humility involved in giving yourself to Him. Just waiting to go to heaven is choosing the wide path. It represents choosing the good life over the life of sacrifice. There is very little death of self in it. Deciding to go to heaven does not make you a Christian. Choosing Jesus over self makes you a Christian.

## The Prudent Man

There is a continual spiritual battle between the spirit of humility and the spirit of pride. Pride wants to control us but we must not allow it to. Humility, however, must control us, because it keeps us on the path of life. In Proverbs 22:3 we read, "A prudent man sees danger and takes refuge, but the simple keep going and suffer for it." All through the Word of God, we see the Lord trying to protect us from the dangers of the wide path. If we look at Proverbs 15:5 we gain more insight into what it is to be prudent: "A fool spurns his father's discipline, but whoever heeds correction shows prudence." In this case to be "prudent" is to be the opposite of the "fool." Those who heed correction, or follow their father's discipline, show prudence.

The prudent man sees danger and takes refuge. God is our refuge. The prudent man will not walk the wide path. However, because of that choice, he must go into His God (refuge) for protection against all the ridicule he will face for choosing the narrow path. Going into God has to do with a continual dying to self. It describes the prayer life. It describes the crucified life. Facing the ridicule and accepting it develops humility within. The meek are people who are willing to obey God. Complete obedience to God develops a meek, prudent, or humble spirit. God in essence, becomes the protector of the meek.

In Proverbs 2:8 we read, "For he guards the course of the just and protects the way of his faithful ones." What is it God protects us from? He protects us from the snares of the world. One problem we face is that we want to live the way we choose, which indicates pride, and when things don't go right we ask God to come and protect us. The problem with that is, God's protection comes through humility because humility is obedience. Humility indicates a complete reliance upon God.

Consider Proverbs 22:4: "Humility and the fear of the Lord bring wealth and honor and life." The proud will not put their life in complete obedience to God. They will not follow the narrow path because of the humility needed to do so. When I first gave my life to Christ, I lived in a house with some other young men. Our house was known as a party house. It was located on the edge of town, and beer parties were the norm each weekend.

After I surrendered my life to Christ, I found it very difficult to continue to live in that house. During the parties (which I had previously participated in) I would go to my room and close the door. I would then sit in my room and listen to the ridicule that would come from the other side of the door. It is not an easy thing to purposely do things that make you unpopular; it's humbling. However, I also found the presence of God to be very real in those times. As I closed myself in with Jesus, I found a quality of spiritual life that I had never known before. There was true wealth, honor, and life in my decision to choose the narrow path.

## The Path of the Wicked

In Proverbs 22:5 we read, "In the paths of the wicked lie thorns and snares, but he who guards his soul stays far from them." In the path of the wicked, the wide path, there are snares. They are things that can entrap us. The snares actually represent the things of the world. In this world, the only thing that is progressive is the Church. The world does not progress toward God. It is quite evident that the world has been on a path of digression for some time, as far as spiritual things are concerned. At best, the world is at a spiritual standstill. The Church is to be in a continual progressive spiritual state. The Word of God often refers to the Church as being on a path toward God. As long as we stay on the narrow path, we continue to progress. When we get close to the side of the road or when we widen the path we are on, we tend to get ensnared or entrapped.

## The Path of the Righteous

It's in this light that we need to consider Proverbs 22:6: "Train a child in the way he should go, and when he is old he will not turn from it." To train a child, in the Hebrew language, deals with disciplining a child in the narrow path. It literally means to narrow up their path continually. The way we "narrow" the path is to hedge it up with thorns. If the child's path is hedged with thorns he will be compelled to stay on it. In other words a parent is not to allow the child to develop a close association with the world, for it will ensnare them. It will hold them back from continuing to progress toward God. The word-picture for being snared is like a sheep getting it's wool caught in the thorns.

I have heard preachers refer to themselves as encouragers. They will make statements like, "I am not a sheep-shearer, I am an encourager." They tend to make sheep shearing out to be something negative. What they are saying, in essence, is that they never preach against sin. They only encourage the sheep. If you think this through even a little you begin to understand the need to shear the sheep periodically. When the wool gets too thick it tends to get caught in the thickets. The thickets, or thorns, represent the world. If the sheep are not sheared once in a while they get caught up in the world. Therefore, sheep shearing is one of the most encouraging and loving things one could do for the sheep because it keeps them on the narrow path.

## *Good Soldiers*

In light of all this, we must now go back to our opening verse, 2 Timothy 2:4-5.

> No one serving as a soldier gets involved in civilian affairs — he wants to please his commanding officer. Similarly, if anyone competes as an athlete, he does not receive the victor's crown unless he competes according to the rules.

In spiritual battle our objective, as God's warriors, is to please our commanding officer. Our commanding officer is Jesus. In order to please Him, we cannot get involved in civilian affairs. We must also participate according to the rules. There are two rules for the warrior. He must serve, and he must not get involved, which means he must not get entangled in the world.

The first requirement is that he must serve. To serve deals with the death of self. It means to endure, or war. The Greek meaning signifies being involved (in this battle) at one's own expense. This means there is a price that must be paid to be involved. Since this is dealing with spiritual battle, it is not talking about a monetary price, but rather a spiritual sacrifice. The sacrifice is self. The only way to war, endure, or serve, is to pay the price of death to self. You serve as a good soldier at the expense of yourself.

Death to self means to live entirely for Christ. The only things Satan can get hold of in a person's life are the things he has not put to death. Everything that is dead is free from satanic influence. That does not mean a person will never experience an attack from the enemy. It simply means that the attack will not threaten a person's spiritual life because there is nothing for Satan to attach himself to.

The second thing God's warrior must do to compete according to the rules, is to not get involved in civil (worldly) affairs. Civil affairs are the entanglement of everyday life that lead to the denial of Christ. The deeper we get into the world, the more we must deny Christ. What exactly is the world? Basically it's the exaltation of man. Worldliness is not much more than man building himself up in the eyes of other men. To live for Christ means you deny yourself. If you do not deny self, you will deny Christ.

God's warrior cannot be involved in worldly affairs. The Greek meaning for "involved or entangled" in this verse is similar to the word "train" from Proverbs 22:6, which we looked at earlier. Both of them deal with a sheep getting his wool caught in thorns. If we are entangled in worldly affairs, we cannot please our commanding officer. One concern I have in regard to the current spiritual warfare emphasis in the church today is that we are trying to engage in spiritual battle while still deeply involved in worldliness. We must compete according to the rules or we disqualify ourselves. We must serve (endure), which is dying to self. We must not entangle, which is humbling ourselves.

## Authority

Consider this — all Satan has is authority. He is the prince of this world. "Now is the time for judgment on this world; now the prince of this world will be driven out" (John 12:31). As believers we are not to be of this world. As long as we stay clear of Satan's world and its entanglements we have authority over him. When we involve ourselves in Satan's world we lose our authority because he is the prince of this world.

We need to learn something about authority. It comes

from position. Often we think authority comes through some physical manifestation. We tend to think that if we are loud or aggressive or forceful we have authority. That is not always the case. We could learn a lot from the local police. A policeman understands authority. He knows that his authority comes from the position he has been granted. With his badge and uniform, he knows he has the backing of the government from the mayor on down.

Suppose a policeman stops your car and wants you to get out of the car. Typically they don't stand beside your car, get all red in the face, and then start screaming at the top of their lungs, "In the name of this state, get out of the car!" They know that is not necessary because of the authority they have. They also know that authority comes through the position they have, not through how loud they yell or through how mad they get. They understand that they could simply say, very calmly, "Get out of the car," and they would have the same authority.

Satan has authority in this world because he is its prince. If you live in this world, you are subject to his position of authority. However, we are not to live in this world. Consider Hebrews 11:13: "All these people were still living by faith when they died. They did not receive the things promised; they only saw them and welcomed them from a distance. And they admitted that they were aliens and strangers on earth." We are to live in a completely different realm. In this other realm, Jesus is the prince. In Acts 5:31 we read, "God exalted him to his own right hand as Prince and Savior that he might give repentance and forgiveness of sins to Israel."

## Our Position

Our position as Christians is that we are "in Christ." "Now if we are children, then we are heirs — heirs of God and co-heirs with Christ, if indeed we share in his sufferings in order that we may also share in his glory"

(Rom. 8:17). We are co-heirs with Christ. Jesus is the prince of God's world. As long as we continue to dwell in His world, we remain in authority over the prince of this world (Satan). We become subject to the prince of whatever world we live in. If we are to compete, if we are to actually engage in spiritual battle, we must compete according to the rules. One of those rules is that God's warrior must live in God's world.

It is very popular today to think of God's warrior in a very physical frame of mind. We take the Ephesians 6 description of the armor of God and create pictures in our minds of a knight in shining armor. In that frame of mind, we are imagining ourselves going out and conquering whole cities for Christ. The point is, we don't have to take a city for Christ. We simply have to exemplify Christ. "Better a patient man than a warrior, a man who controls his temper than one who takes a city" (Prov. 16:32). God's warrior is one who walks as Christ walked. Demons tremble at our obedience to Christ, not at our feeble attempt to cut their heads off with the sword of the Lord. We cannot kill demons, we can only make them subject to operate in their own realm. Their realm is the heart of the unregenerate man, which is where the world is. When we bring an unregenerate man into regeneration, Satan loses his influence because we have taken him out from under the authority of the prince of this world and made him subject to the Prince of Peace.

The issue then becomes that of how do we most effectively bring men into regeneration? We do so by competing according to the rules. To compete according to the rules is to walk the narrow path. It is to walk as Jesus walked. It is to live in Christ's world.

# Chapter 4

# Who Does God Think He Is?

It is impossible to be a spiritual leader or even a good soldier for the Lord without a right attitude. David once prayed, "Create in me a pure heart, O God, and renew a steadfast spirit within me" (Ps. 51:10). A steadfast spirit or a right spirit is just as important as a pure heart. Without a right spirit your heart will not stay pure for very long.

"Your attitude should be the same as that of Christ Jesus" (Phil. 2:5). Paul admonishes us to have a Christlike attitude. A Christ-like attitude is a servant attitude. "But made himself nothing, taking the very nature of a servant, being made in human likeness" (Phil. 2:7). A true servant seeks no self-glory. He has one desire only — to give his life for the master. "And being found in appearance as a man, he humbled himself and became obedient to death — even death on a cross!" (Phil. 2:8).

Those who struggle with the idea of servanthood are typically those who want to be served rather than to serve. When you desire to be served you ultimately struggle with God's authority in your life.

## Don't Interfere with Me, God!

"Keep falsehood and lies far from me; give me neither poverty nor riches, but give me only my daily bread. Otherwise, I may have too much and disown you and say, 'Who is the Lord?' Or I may become poor and steal, and so dishonor the name of my God," (Prov. 30:8-9). These two verses fairly accurately describe a very divisive attitude in the Church today. This attitude is a very defiant one that says, "Just who does God think He is; interfering with my life?"

This attitude has been in the world for some time. However, that is not such a problem. An unregenerate man's view of God isn't nearly as important as the regenerate man's view is. God understands that if a man is spiritually blind he will never see correctly. The problem is not in how the world views God, it's in how the Church views God. There is a prevailing thought in the Church today that says, "What right does God have to intervene in my life?"

It is very common today for a pastor to be counseling someone in need of help. In giving advice he will lay out the biblical path a person should take. It is becoming more and more common for the person's reaction to be something like, "That may be what the Bible says, but it's not what I'm going to do."

I remember a situation in my own life where I was counseling a couple who were seeking God's direction concerning a problem they faced. It was a situation where the Word of God was very clear. I directed them to God's Word and said, "Here is your only option."

Their response shocked me when they said, "We will need to pray about what we are going to do."

I said, "What are you going to ask God for in prayer?"

They said, "We will pray for direction."

I said, "God has already given you direction through His Word. The problem is not that you need direction. You already have that. Your problem is that you do not want to listen to what God has already told you through His Word."

It is impossible to be sincere in prayer if you are praying something contrary to what God has already clearly defined in His Word. Basically what this couple was saying was, "We know what we want for our lives and we don't want God to intervene or interfere." The Church today has lost a sense of the holiness and majesty of God. When we lose sight of who God really is we tend to focus in on ourselves, and who we are.

## Who Is God?

"In the year that King Uzziah died, I saw the Lord seated on a throne, high and exalted, and the train of his robe filled the temple. Above him were seraphs, each with six wings: With two wings they covered their faces, with two they covered their feet, and with two they were flying. And they were calling to one another: 'Holy, holy, holy is the Lord Almighty; the whole earth is full of his glory.' At the sound of their voices the doorposts and thresholds shook and the temple was filled with smoke. 'Woe to me!' I cried. 'I am ruined! For I am a man of unclean lips, and I live among a people of unclean lips, and my eyes have seen the King, the Lord Almighty' " (Isa. 6:1-5). When Isaiah stood before the Lord he was overwhelmed. He felt he was not even worthy to be in His presence.

From the lack of prayer in our lives we have lost a true living sense of who God is. The practice of prayer is what keeps us separated from the philosophies of this world. The separation that comes through that is the avenue to holiness. Holiness means to be separated. The word "sanctification" is very similar in its meaning to the word "holiness." In either case separation from the world, or living apart from its theories so that you can give yourself over to the thought processes of the Holy Spirit, is what develops a holy lifestyle within us. Prayer keeps us focusing in on who God really is. When we keep that in proper perspective we develop a proper balance in life.

### King Nebuchadnezzar

Let's consider King Nebuchadnezzar. In the book of Daniel we can learn some very important lessons about keeping a right perspective on who God really is. "I, Nebuchadnezzar, was at home in my palace, *contented and prosperous*" (Dan. 4:4). Do you remember what Solomon's warning was about being contented and prosperous? He said our tendency is to say, "Who is the Lord?" (Prov. 30:9).

"I had a dream that made me afraid. As I was lying in my bed, the images and visions that passed through my mind terrified me" (Dan. 4:5). It is significant that the king could not interpret the dream himself. Whenever we are contented and prosperous we tend to lose the cutting edge of our relationship with God. We get fat and sassy and then when we are called to a spiritual exercise, there is nothing for us to draw from. The Scripture teaches us that in the midst of carnal comfort we lose our desire to fight. In America it seems we don't really want to do anything about inflation as long as we can just keep getting pay raises. Samson lost his desire to defend his own commitment to God because of the carnal comfort Delilah afforded him.

"So I commanded that all the wise men of Babylon be brought before me to interpret the dream for me. When the magicians, enchanters, astrologers and diviners came, I told them the dream, but they could not interpret it for me. Finally, Daniel came into my presence and I told him the dream. . . . I said, "Belteshazzar, chief of the magicians, I know that the spirit of the holy gods is in you, and no mystery is too difficult for you. Here is my dream; interpret it for me" (Dan. 4:6-9).

None of the king's men, those who followed his pattern of life, could discern this spiritual event. Finally Daniel comes along. Daniel is a spiritual man. Daniel even refused to eat the king's delicacies. He had a cutting edge in his relationship with God. It is significant that the king recognized that the spirit of the Holy God was in Daniel.

"This is the interpretation, O king, and this is the decree the Most High has issued against my lord the king: You will be driven away from people and will live with the wild animals; you will eat grass like cattle and be drenched with the dew of heaven. Seven times will pass by for you until you acknowledge that the Most High is sovereign over the kingdoms of men and gives them to anyone he wishes. The command to leave the stump of the tree with its roots means that your kingdom will be restored to you when you acknowledge that Heaven rules" (Dan. 4:24-26).

King Nebuchadnezzar had come to the place of questioning why he needed God, so great was the splendor of his kingdom. Daniel tells him that because of that attitude God was going to bring him down and cause him to live beneath men until he came to the place of acknowledging the holiness of God and that it is God who rules over the affairs of men.

Then in verse 27 Daniel gives him one last bit of advice: "Therefore, O king, be pleased to accept my advice: Renounce your sins by doing what is right, and your wickedness by being kind to the oppressed. It may be that then your prosperity will continue." Even in light of all the glory King Nebuchadnezzar had taken upon himself, God was still going to give him another opportunity to repent. "Renounce your sins." That's mercy! Did the king receive this advice. No! Why? Because he had lost a true sense of the holiness and majesty of God.

## Our Current Dilemma

Here is the dilemma many pastors face today. The pastor is called in to interpret a problem. The parishioner has heard that the Spirit of God resides in his pastor so he asks him for direction. The pastor then gives advice based on the written Word of God. He gives strict warnings! He says something like, "You must change your ways. You must repent! If you don't you will ultimately live beneath men." So the warning is given. Is it heeded? Only if there is a great respect for who God is. If the person has been living a life of contentment and prosperity it probably will go unheeded because he has lost the cutting edge in his relationship with God. I have talked with many pastors who tell me the same thing. They say they no longer counsel their own people because it seems that almost without exception everyone they counsel eventually leaves their church.

After Daniel gave his advice (really God's advice) the king did nothing with it. God gave him a whole year to change his ways but he didn't. We pick up this account one year later "Twelve months later, as the king was walking on the roof of the royal palace of Babylon, he said, 'Is not this the great Babylon I have built as the royal residence, by my mighty power and for the glory of my majesty?' " (Dan. 4:29-30).

That was the final blow. After all of God's attempts to bring him to repentance, the king still believes he can live his life outside of God's control. Consider what happens next. "The words were still on his lips when a voice came from heaven, 'This is what is decreed for you, King

Nebuchadnezzar: Your royal authority has been taken from you. You will be driven away from people and will live with the wild animals; you will eat grass like cattle. Seven times will pass by for you until you acknowledge that the Most High is sovereign over the kingdoms of men and gives them to anyone he wishes' " (Dan. 4:31-32).

Taking glory from God is basically that of believing you are the source of your own success. When you believe that it is *your* talent and *your* ability that has brought you success you set yourself up for a fall. All the Lord was trying to do was to cause King Nebuchadnezzar to see that He is sovereign, and that He gave the king his kingdom. Nebuchadnezzar had come to believe that he built Babylon himself. All through the Word we see God directing His attention to His shepherds. When the shepherds fully acknowledge God they tend to lead the sheep toward Him. When the shepherds develop pride they tend to cause people to worship them.

The king spent seven years in the wilderness. Then we read, "At the end of that time, I, Nebuchadnezzar, raised my eyes toward heaven, and my sanity was restored. Then I praised the Most High; I honored and glorified him who lives forever. His dominion is an eternal dominion; his kingdom endures from generation to generation" (Dan. 4:34). His sanity was restored when he praised, honored, and glorified the Most High.

"Now I, Nebuchadnezzar, praise and exalt and glorify the King of heaven, because everything he does is right and all his ways are just. And those who walk in pride he is able to humble" (Dan. 4:37). God is able to humble those who walk in pride. For many years Nebuchadnezzar was saying, "Who is the Lord?" Now he is saying, "He is Lord!" God will share His glory with no man. If we get to the place where we can just shake off the godly advice of others we put ourselves in a position of being humbled. "But he gives us more grace. That is why Scripture says: 'God opposes the proud but gives grace to the humble' " (James 4:6). Humble yourself in the sight of the Lord. Line up your life with His Word. Do what He tells you to do.

## But I Tell You

There is something very interesting about the phrase "But I tell you." There are many times when Christ used this phrase to counter the philosophies of man. However, the nature of this phrase indicates a debate is taking place. The setting could be something like this: Jesus is discussing the issues of life with a man when the man begins to express his opinions about the same issues. Jesus counters him by saying, "That may be how you see it; but I tell you this." In other words the discussion should be over when Jesus expresses His heart over the matter. However, today we don't just take His advice. We weigh His advice against our own feelings about things and then make a decision based on how we see things. This is wrong!

This addresses the issue of the lordship of Christ. Someone once said, "Jesus is either Lord of all, or not at all." Jesus cannot be Lord of some of your life. He is either your Lord or He isn't. His lordship is largely established by how you react to this little phrase; "But I tell you." If Jesus is Lord of your life, then when He says, "But I tell you," the discussion is over. For instance when Jesus says, "But I tell you that men will have to give account on the day of judgment for every careless word they have spoken" (Matt. 12:36), we are confronted with whether or not we will stop using careless words. If you have a "Who is the Lord?" attitude, you will make all types of excuses as to why you will continue to use careless words. If you have a "Jesus is Lord" attitude, then when Jesus says, "But I tell you, don't use careless words," the discussion is over. You no longer try to justify the use of them.

Jesus was setting the stage to establish himself as Lord in the hearts of men while He was on earth. He did this in large measure by countering their traditions and showing them how their own perception of things needed to conform to His. This is why we often read in the Gospels Jesus saying, "You have heard that it was said." Then He counters it with, "But I tell you." He was trying to establish the preeminence of God's Word over their own word.

"You have heard that it was said," is a phrase that addresses the traditions of men and the reasoning of men. In order to institute His lordship men would need to leave their own reasoning behind and follow the Lord based on what the Lord knows and says, not on what man knows. Some of these sayings are hard sayings. Consider the next few verses, "You have heard that it was said to the people long ago, 'Do not murder, and anyone who murders will be subject to judgment.' But I tell you that anyone who is angry with his brother will be subject to judgment. Again, anyone who says to his brother, 'Raca,' is answerable to the Sanhedrin. But anyone who says, 'You fool!' will be in danger of the fire of hell" (Matt. 5:21-22). Many times we believe our anger is justified and we tend to overlook these verses. When we believe we are justified we often base that on the traditions and philosophies of men. On that premise we often ignore His words, "But I tell you."

## *He Is Lord!*

Who does God think He is? He thinks He is Lord, and so should we. He is Lord! "If we have been united with him like this in his death, we will certainly also be united with him in his resurrection" (Rom. 6:5). The proof that we have been through the crucifixion with Jesus is that we have a definite likeness to Him. If we have been planted together in the likeness of His death, if we have put to death our sinful nature, then we shall be in the likeness of His righteousness. If we have the resurrection life of Jesus within us, it will show itself in true holiness. One of Christ's most notable characteristics was His unwavering obedience to His father.

If Jesus is Lord of your life it will manifest itself in your own unwavering obedience to Him. If we were to cross-examine our own obedience to God we may find that it doesn't measure up. Something has happened in the Church to where it is very difficult to find living examples of the lordship of Christ. Gone are the days when we would abstain from worldly entertainment. Christians today will watch the Oscars on TV for three hours straight and then complain when their pastor's sermon goes more than 30 minutes. Gone are the days when we thought the world's standards of living were below the life of the Christian. Today the world sets our standards for fashion, and it determines our activities and our music.

Gone are the days when the people of God spent time in the presence of God in prayer. Gone are the days when God was the object of our affection. Gone are the days of doing everything possible to bring our neighbors to Christ through the life we live before them.

Gone also are the Shekinah days when the presence of God brought us to our knees, and the spirit of God convicted us, and the fire of God consumed us. We no longer come to church to meet with God. We no longer come to be bowled over with the majesty of His presence. We come to hear sermons about God. We want sermons that do not interfere with the way we want to live. We preach far more psychology than anything else.

God, don't give us poverty. Don't give us riches. Give us that which is our portion so that our dependence will always be on You. Father, we never want to be guilty of saying, "Who is the Lord? And why does He think He can run our lives?" Instead let our prayer be, "Jesus, be the Lord of all."

# PART TWO

# Spiritual Husbands

# Chapter 5

# Husbands, Love Your Wives!

I was once counseling with a couple in Ogden, Utah. They came to me after I finished speaking in their church and asked if I would meet with them the next day. I told them I would, so we set up an appointment in the church.

Their case was not uncommon. The wife was complaining that her husband never showed her any affection and that he constantly did things to purposely annoy her. I asked the husband if what she said was true.

He said, "Yes."

I said, "You mean you purposely do things that you know annoy her?"

Again he said, "Yes."

I sat there rather stunned by his lack of concern and said, "Why? If you know that she is bothered by certain things why would you want to make it uncomfortable for her."

Finally he said, "I do these things because I know she will always forgive me. She needs me."

I had never heard anyone put it that way before.

However, I am sure he is not the only man that does this type of thing. I said to him, "Do you mean to tell me that you are justifying your actions based on your wife's love for you?"

He said, "You could say that."

I then said to him, "Why don't you turn things around and start doing things based on your love for your wife instead of her love for you?"

If we do things based on our love for others we will then do things the way we would want them done to us.

How would we feel as a part of the bride of Christ if Jesus mistreated us based on our love for Him? Suppose Jesus understood that we needed Him in order to make it to heaven one day and so He continually abused us knowing that we would ultimately forgive Him. He wouldn't be much of a Saviour, would He? It is very typical for men to treat their wives in ways that they would never want to be treated. Jesus will never mistreat us because He bases His actions toward us on His love for us, not on our love for Him.

### Did God Reject His People?

Consider the following verses. "I ask then: Did God reject His people? By no means! I am an Israelite myself, a descendant of Abraham, from the tribe of Benjamin" (Rom. 11:1). Did God reject His people? The reason this question was asked is found in Romans 11:8: "As it is written: 'God gave them a spirit of stupor, eyes so that they could not see and ears so that they could not hear, to this very day.' " If God gave Israel a spirit of stupor, so that she could not "see" or "hear," we would logically conclude that God did this so that Israel would fall and be lost forever. However, that was not God's plan.

Paul tells us God's plan in Romans 11:11: "Again I ask: Did they stumble so as to fall beyond recovery? Not at all! Rather, because of their transgression, salvation has come to the Gentiles to make Israel envious."

I remember hearing Bill Gothard teach on this in one of his "Basic Youth Conflict" seminars. He said, "Israel is God's spiritual wife. Out of the union between God and Israel a son was born, Jesus Christ." Israel is currently a wayward wife. She has not responded to the wooings of the Lord. She has rejected even her own Son. "He came to that which was his own, but his own did not receive him" (John 1:11). Even though Jesus came to His own people and they rejected Him, God is still working at bringing them back to Him.

God will not give up on His rebellious wife. Subsequently, He gave her a spirit of stupor causing her to reject her son as the Messiah, so that salvation could come to the Gentiles.

If Israel had not rejected the Messiah, He would never have been sent to the cross to die for our sins. Because Jesus died for us, we now can have a very intimate relationship with Him. Our relationship with Christ is supposed to make Israel, or the world, envious. God is trying to provoke Israel back to himself through jealousy. The whole idea behind this is that Israel is to see the beauty of our relationship with the Lord and want it for herself. To put it another way, the world has tried everything and still has no answers for her problems. Ideally, she will one day see our relationship with the Lord and become envious of us.

### Divorce

God's spiritual wife has left Him. However, God will not give up on her. He is doing all He can to bring her back to Him. God will not give up, and neither can we. You may be facing a very difficult situation in your marriage. God's word to you is, "Don't give up." When men give us that advice we often respond by saying,

"That's easy for you to say, but you don't know what I'm going through!" That's true! But God does know, and He says, "Don't give up!"

I remember a man coming to me once with a marriage problem. He said, "My wife wants a divorce and I have decided to give it to her because that is her will." He continued to say, "I believe I should grant her her will."

I answered him by saying, "I don't believe your wife's will should be the ultimate thing giving you direction, but rather God's will. What is God's will in the matter? Follow that!"

He had already made up his mind and eventually granted her a divorce. The man was using his wife's will as an excuse to do what he wanted to do anyway.

I need to say a few words about divorce at this point. First we must look to the Word of God. "I hate divorce," says the Lord God of Israel" (Mal. 2:16). Obviously God hates divorce; however, God does not hate the divorcee. To think that God hates the divorcee would be to say that God hates the sinner as much as the sin.

Husbands and wives represent Christ and the Church, respectively. " 'For this reason a man will leave his father and mother and be united to his wife, and the two will become one flesh.' This is a profound mystery — but I am talking about Christ and the church" (Eph. 5:31-32). When husbands and wives divorce, it is symbolic of Christ and the Church going their separate ways. God hates what it symbolizes, but He doesn't hate those who go through it. God is in the business of rebuilding. He is interested in reconstructing the lives of those who have gone through a divorce. What we are dealing with here is meant to be preventative medicine. The divorced person would be the first one to want to keep others from going through the same hurt they have gone through. That is all this is meant to be.

### Solution without Sacrifice?

God never offers a solution without some kind of sacrifice on His own part. Solution without sacrifice develops into apathy — it's ungodly. All of God's solutions for our problems come through His own sacrifice. If God is telling us to hang in there and to go through this tough time, it's because that is exactly what He is doing at this time.

When I was in Bible college, I worked part-time for a large corporation. I was working in the payroll department, running the computers that processed the checks. I worked at a regional office where we would generate the payroll for over 13,000 employees. There were some executives in this company who were making some rather large salaries. We would process checks for $50,000 and $70,000. Attached to those checks was mine for $125.00. After a while, I began to get a little upset. It appeared that I was keeping these other people successful without any sacrifice on their part. I became apathetic.

One day the Lord spoke to me while I was reading Ephesians 6:5-7: "Slaves, obey your earthly masters with respect and fear, and with sincerity of heart, just as you would obey Christ. Obey them not only to win their favor when their eye is on you, but like slaves of Christ, doing the will of God from your heart. Serve wholeheartedly, as if you were serving the Lord, not men."

When I read that first word, "slaves," I knew this applied to me. Then I read how we should go about our jobs as if we were serving Christ, and not mere man. This convicted me because I had become bitter towards my boss. Finally God said, "Ron, you need to die to this situation. You have focused too much on yourself. Just die to it." Do you know why God could offer that solution? It's because it comes through His own sacrifice. Jesus can ask us to die to any situation because long before He ever asked us to die, He died. His solution for my problem came through His own sacrifice.

### Rights Conscious

One of the great problems in America today is that we have become rights-conscious and not responsibility-conscious. This has even filtered into the Church. Christians have focused much more on what it means to be a King's kid than on what it means to reveal the King to others. The whole abortion issue has become a rights issue rather than a responsibility issue.

Men, you may have your wife dead-to-rights as far as the biblical qualifications for divorce are concerned, but you also have a responsibility. A "rights-focus" comes from a heart of stone. A "responsibility-focus" comes from a heart of flesh. When you took Jesus into your heart, He was to have taken your heart of stone and given you a heart of flesh. "I will give you a new heart and put a new spirit in you; I will remove from you your heart of stone and give you a heart of flesh" (Ezek. 36:26). This is what the Bible addresses in Matthew 19:8: "Jesus replied, 'Moses permitted you to divorce your wives because your hearts were hard. But it was not this way from the beginning.' "

If we were to look strictly at the issue of rights, how many of us would have a right to salvation? One of the biblical qualifications for divorce is that of adultery. However, every one of us has committed spiritual adultery. In other words, God has each of us dead-to-rights, yet He looks beyond His rights to His responsibility and says in essence, "I have a responsibility to my Son to forgive those who ask for forgiveness, even though I have every right to send them into eternal damnation." God has every right to put us away, yet He forgives. If we continue to believe that we have a right to put our wife away because she has violated the marriage vows, that's hardhearted! It's not loving them the way Christ loves us.

We could all learn more about forgiveness. I remember talking to a woman once about her marriage. She was expressing to me that things were not going very well. In the course of our conversation, she mentioned that many years prior, she had caught her husband in an adulterous affair. As we continued to talk, I asked her if she was planning to use his affair as the means for a divorce. She looked at me quite surprised and said, "Heavens no! I forgave him of that. That means it's as though it never happened. I could never divorce him over something I have forgiven him of, or it would be like never having forgiven him."

I must say I was quite surprised. I hadn't run into that type of Christianity for some time. Can you imagine what would happen in our society if we actually treated others the way Christ treats us?

## Husband's Main Objective

A husband's main objective in life should be that of offering up to Jesus a bride without spot or wrinkle. The husband represents Christ. Christ is spending all of His time preparing a bride. The whole work of the Church is that of maturing, preparing, and prepping the bride. One day Jesus will stand before His Father and say in essence, "Father, here is what I have done with what You have given Me. Here is My bride without spot or wrinkle."

"Husbands, love your wives, just as Christ loved the church and gave himself up for her to make her holy, cleansing her by the washing with water through the word, and to present her to himself as a radiant church, without stain or wrinkle or any other blemish, but holy and blameless" (Eph. 5:25-27).

Ephesians 5:28 begins by saying, "In this same way, husbands ought to love their wives." That little phrase, "In the same way," refers to the same way that Christ loves the Church and is preparing her to present her to the Father. Husbands, this indicates that one day we will do something similar. One day we will stand before the Lord and say, "Here is what I have done with what you have given me. Here is my bride." Will she be without spot or wrinkle? Are you cleansing her with the Word? Will she be radiant? Nothing could surpass that. However, in order for that to come true you may have to give up all your rights. You have a responsibility to God and to your family.

In order to help your family develop in the things of God, you may have to give up everything. However, how much did Christ love His bride? He loved her so much that He gave himself to her and died for her. The one man who could have exercised His rights without anyone criticizing Him, gave them up completely. When we exercise our rights over our responsibilities, we exalt ourselves over and above Christ.

The problem most men have is that they haven't fully submitted to the new nature they received when they accepted Christ into their hearts. The Bible tells us that if a man is in Christ all things become new. Jesus gives us a new nature, He gives us His nature. His nature is to ultimately control us. His nature is to die for others. It takes humility to allow others to defeat you, but through the defeat victory comes.

Jesus was dead for three days then He was resurrected into new life. Typically, when we die to something there is a time when things don't look so good. However, if we will endure, new life will come. God won't allow those who die for others to stay dead. He brings His life to them. When you have life from God you are fulfilled, even if your situation hasn't yet changed.

## *Reward!*

What reward could surpass that of seeing our whole family stand before God, clean? A few years ago there was a book written called *Better than Heaven, and Worse than Hell.* Typically we think of heaven as being the best and hell being the worst. How could you get better or worse than these two things? The idea behind the book was this: That which is better than heaven itself is going there and then finding out that by the example you set, your whole family is going to follow you there. That which is worse than hell itself is that of going there and then finding out that by the example you set, your whole family is going to follow you there.

A husband's main objective in life should be to develop his wife. The reason for that was described in one of our opening verses. "Salvation has come to the Gentiles to make Israel envious" (Rom. 11:11). God is going to draw Israel to himself through provoking her to jealousy. This is why Jesus gives all of His attention to the Church. If the Church was fully mature in the things of God, she would have a great effect on this world. If the Church was truly moving with the Spirit of God, it would be provoking millions to her. The world would begin to want what we have. She would become jealous of what we have.

The Church of Jesus Christ should have the strongest marriages and families in the world. If we had all that we should, the world would literally be knocking down the doors of the Church, saying, "We are envious of what you have." The world has tried everything it can think of to save the family and it has no answers. Everything it has tried has failed. The only hope for the family today is Christ. Jesus has always been the answer and always will be the answer.

Strong marriages and families can become the greatest evangelistic tool we have today. That is why a husband's main objective in life should be developing his wife and family. This comes before evangelism and then actually becomes evangelism. We have a tremendous responsibility to God and the world to show them what the Son of God can do for them.

# Chapter 6

# *Priests of the Home*

Most men don't feel like priests, yet the Bible says we are. We are priests in our own homes. We have a little congregation also, it's our families. It may be small but it is the most important congregation we will ever preside over.

Consider the following verses concerning our priesthood. First Peter 2:5 says, "You also, like living stones, are being built into a spiritual house to be a holy priesthood, offering spiritual sacrifices acceptable to God through Jesus Christ." The Scripture declares that we are being built into a spiritual house so that we can function in the role of priests. God's desire is that one day we would reign with Christ. "You have made them to be a kingdom and priests to serve our God, and they will reign on the earth" (Rev. 5:10). What we begin to understand from this is that this life is like a training ground for the life to come. The things we allow God to teach us today will have eternal benefits. First Peter 2:5 is directed to the whole bride of Christ which is made up of both men and women. However, when it comes to the home, the husband is appointed as the priest.

In Ephesians 5:23-24 we read, "For the husband is the head of the wife as Christ is the head of the church, his body, of which he is the Savior. Now as the church submits to Christ, so also wives should submit to their husbands in everything" (Eph. 5:23-24). Paul teaches us here that men have a responsibility as ambassadors of Christ, to consider what Jesus would do and then pattern their lives after Him. Men are the priests of their home, but all of their direction is to come from their own High Priest, Jesus. We have no freedom to make decisions or to even give directions apart from the guidance that our High Priest gives us.

## Chosen

We will gain much more insight into this issue from the Book of Hebrews. In Hebrews 5:1 we read, "Every high priest is selected from among men and is appointed to represent them in matters related to God, to offer gifts and sacrifices for sins." This comes from the Old Testament practice we find in Leviticus 21:10 which says, "The high priest, the one among his brothers who has had the anointing oil poured on his head and who has been ordained to wear the priestly garments, must not let his hair become unkempt or tear his clothes." It states that the high priest was picked from among his brethren. He was chosen and anointed.

In the home, God has appointed the husband to fulfill this role. The husband, therefore, is chosen by God from amongst his brethren, his family, to be the priest. He is appointed on behalf of his family to preside over the divine worship of the home. In other words, he is to reign over all of those things that pertain to the personal salvation of his family members. He does this so that he can qualify in offering both gifts and sacrifices for sin.

Don't confuse this with the ultimate offering for sin that Christ made on the cross. This is simply addressing the husband's responsibility as the high priest of the home.

## The Revelation of God

God has always appeared to men in two basic ways: (1) He has appeared as the author and dispenser of all temporal goods, and (2) He has appeared as the lawgiver and the judge. That is also how the husband or father is to appear to his family. Traditionally speaking, the man is the breadwinner. I realize that in our society things have developed to the point where many women must also work. In some cases the woman makes as much money as her husband, or even more money than him. That, however, does not change the man's God-given role. Neither does it change his position or the call on his life. There is something about the position of the man that causes him to be viewed naturally as the provider of the home.

The man is also the one who usually administers or enforces the laws or rules of the household. Mom can be an enforcer also, but typically she doesn't carry the same clout as dad does in this matter. As a young boy, I remember many times my mom would have to say something to me that I dreaded very much. I grew up with three brothers. That forced my mom to be an enforcer of the law from time to time. Periodically us boys would simply not obey her. Finally she would say, "Wait until your dad gets home!" None of us boys wanted to hear that.

Have you ever considered why dad's discipline was worse than mom's? I don't believe that it was strictly because he was physically stronger and could spank us harder. With four boys to raise, my mom learned how to use the wooden spoon on us. We dreaded that also, but there was still something about dad spanking us that made it seem worse.

Dads have the God-given role of enforcer. There is a certain clout that goes along with the office that cannot be duplicated by another. I can remember many times my dad disciplining me and all the while he was saying, "Why didn't you obey your mom?" Many times he didn't even know why he was disciplining me, he was simply upset with the fact that I would not obey the one who had authority over me, my mom.

We can understand this better when we look at the Church. The pastor's role in the Church is similar to mom's role in the family. The pastor is the one who has the most physical contact with his congregation, similar to how mom is the one with the most physical contact with the children. Dad is often off working and away from home in the same way that Jesus has gone away to prepare a mansion for us. The pastor gets his direction from his head (Jesus), as to how to deal with the problems he faces in his church. A mom often gains direction and strength from her head, the husband.

If the pastor needs to discipline someone from his congregation and that discipline is heeded, then it has accomplished what it needs to. However, if we will not come under his authority, then God must deal with us. In 1 Corinthians we read of a man who persists in his sin. Paul says that since he won't receive the discipline of the church, you should put him out of the church. "And you are proud! Shouldn't you rather have been filled with grief and have put out of your fellowship the man who did this?" (1 Cor. 5:2). He goes on to say, "Hand this man over to Satan, so that the sinful nature may be destroyed and his spirit saved on the day of the Lord" (1 Cor. 5:5).

Handing a man over to Satan is allowing him to wallow in his sin so that he will ultimately come face to face with his God. We see the same type of thing in the account of the prodigal son. In Luke 15:18 we read of the prodigal's final deduction after having been allowed to pursue his sin, "I will set out and go back to my father and say to him: Father, I have sinned against heaven and against you" (Luke 15:18). Because he had ultimately come to this conclusion one could say that "his spirit was saved on the day of the Lord."

Matthew 21:44 says, "He who falls on this stone will be broken to pieces, but he on whom it falls will be crushed." This gives us some insight as to why dad's discipline is much more severe than mom's. Falling on the stone is like coming under the authority of mom. There is some pain in her discipline. However, if we will not fall on the stone, it will fall on us. Dad represents God. His discipline represents the stone falling on us. If you fall on the stone you will get hurt; if the stone falls on you, you will get crushed.

## High Priests of the Home

Prior to the time of Christ, sacrifices and gifts were brought to the high priest. The people of that day could not offer their own offerings, they had to be brought to the one who had the authority to do so because he alone could bring them to God. The high priest was the mediator between God and the people. So the people would bring gifts and sacrifices to be offered to God on their behalf.

Today we also have a High Priest in Jesus Christ. Therefore, we no longer need to go through man. Jesus offers our gifts and sacrifices to the Father. "Let us then approach the throne of grace with confidence, so that we may receive mercy and find grace to help us in our time of need" (Heb. 4:16). Today we can approach the throne with confidence.

In the home, the earthly father is its high priest. He is to reign over all the things that pertain to the salvation of his family in the same way that Christ reigns over all those things that pertain to our own salvation. Even though his family does not offer gifts and sacrifices to him, he still offers gifts and sacrifices to God for the sake of his family and their salvation. He does this so that they might gain salvation. Their salvation does not come through his actions or offerings. He does not and cannot purchase their salvation. He does it so that they might *come into* their salvation.

"The high priest, the one among his brothers who has had the anointing oil poured on his head and who has been ordained to wear the priestly garments . . ." (Lev. 21:10). He is ordained for men. He is chosen from among men to be an example for men. Dads are not the source of their families' salvation, Christ is, but dads are to be the example of Christ for their families. Paul expressed something similar to this in Philippians 4:9, "Whatever you have learned or received or heard from me, or seen in me — put it into practice. And the God of peace will be with you."

## Offering Gifts

The high priest of the home is to offer gifts for the sake of his family. These gifts can come in the form of tithes and offerings. He wants his family to recognize his God. He knows that God is the supplier of all eternal and temporal needs. If he wants his family to understand that facet of God, then he teaches it through offering his gifts to God. This is as much for his family's sake as it is his own. Dads should tithe to be obedient to God and to be an example to their families. If a man wants his family to know that God is the ultimate supplier, he will give to God his own means of supply (tithe) as an object lesson to them. He wants to teach them to be dependent upon God and not their own talent.

The high priest of the home is to also offer the sacrifice of prayer for his family. Prayer is a true sacrifice in that one must die to self in order to give himself to prayer. Prayer then becomes the sacrifice of self. The high priest of the home is to spend time in prayer for a number of reasons. The primary reason for his prayer life should be the salvation of his family. Consider Jesus, our High Priest: "Therefore he is able to save completely those who come to God through him, because he always lives to intercede for them" (Heb. 7:25). Christ is our source of salvation. This verse says He is able to save us when we come to Him because of His intercession. Jesus lives for the purpose of prayer. He continually offers up to God the sacrifice of himself because of how sinful man still is.

If the high priest of the home is not a man of prayer, he is not worthy of the position. The lack of prayer means the high priest of the home is not reigning over those things that pertain to the salvation of his family. It means he is not properly reigning over the very family that God appointed him to govern. Until every member of a man's family knows Christ, prayer must be the passion of his heart. Even after his own family comes to know Christ fully, prayer is to still remain his passion because of how sinful mankind is and how easy it is to turn from Christ.

## Priests of Mercy

Hebrews 5:2 says, "He is able to deal gently with those who are ignorant and are going astray, since he himself is subject to weakness." Dealing gently has to do with mercy and moderation. The high priest of the home is to deal with each of his family members in relationship to his own ignorance and weakness. Most sin falls under one of two categories: ignorance or weakness. Ignorance does not excuse a man if he has within his grasp the means of instruction.

When the high priest considers the sin of another

man he must consider where that man is in life. He must deal with him according to that man's understanding of God. It is not difficult to get fully disgusted with the sinfulness of man. When we see all that is going on in the world, it is easy to express dismay over it. The Word of God says that the high priest is to deal with those people in accordance to their own ignorance because he, too, is ignorant.

What man among us knows everything? There are many things God knows that we will never know. God deals with us according to our own understanding and experience. It is very easy to get upset with people and want to deal with them in a very condemning way. About that time, the Holy Spirit gently speaks to us and says, "Were it not for the grace of God you would be exactly like them."

I remember a true story about a man and his daughter who were flying on an airplane late one night. It was one of those flights where they turn down the lights so people can sleep. The man's four-year-old daughter would not settle down. She was crying, complaining, and moving around so much that finally someone blurted out, "Can't you make her shut up!"

At that, the dad stood up to address the rest of the passengers. He said, "I apologize for my daughter. She has been having trouble dealing with something that just happened. Two days ago my wife and daughter were with me on vacation. We were driving down the road when we had a terrible accident. My wife is lying in a casket in the cargo bay of this airplane."

God deals with us according to what he knows about us. He knows those things you have been subject to that you had no control over. It is not uncommon today to find adults who had horrendous childhoods. The reason God can so easily forgive us is because He understands us. He knows what is in the cargo bay of our lives. This is why a man with a very sinful past can simply say, "God, have mercy on me," and it's done in an instant.

## Priests with Clay Feet

The high priests of the home are men of ignorance and weakness, yet God has appointed them to this position. Because of their own weakness, they are to deal with other men according to what they (the high priests) understand about themselves and according to what others understand about God. If a teenager takes his hand and knocks his plate of food off the table because he doesn't like what mom cooked, you would deal differently with him than you would if a one-year-old knocked his plate off the table. We are to deal with them with mercy and moderation.

When I came to Christ, God had mercy on me. He did not make me pay the price of my own sin. However, having now come into a knowledge of Him, with the eyes of my understanding being enlightened, I reap what I sow. We must understand the difference between the truth of mercy and the mercy of truth. To the one who is unenlightened or ignorant, the truth of mercy is applied. God completely forgives us because we were ignorant. After we experience the new birth and we begin to grow in the Lord, the mercy of truth is applied. There is mercy in revealing truth. The initial revelation of truth appears harsh, but when God causes us to face the penalty of our sin, we tend to turn from it. God never reveals truth for any reason other than to reconcile us unto himself.

This is not much different than when we are forced to discipline our own children. As a father, I take no personal pleasure in correcting my son, except for the fact of knowing that making him come face to face with his sinfulness will cause him to turn from it. To never discipline our children would be a lack of mercy. To allow them to live in error would be a great disservice to them.

The other category for sin is weakness. The great majority of the human race sins through weakness of the flesh. The principle of evil is strong in men. Occasions for sin are many. However, weakness is no excuse when the means for strength is at hand.

The reason the high priest should be slow to punish and prone to forgive is that he himself is beset with weakness. It's much easier to be hard on someone else's child than your own. The reason for that is because you view your own children and their problems from understanding your own problems. You understand that your own problems have had an influence on them. Because of that, you deal with them a little more gently.

These two circumstances, ignorance and weakness, were all considered by the Jewish high priest and should continue to be a consideration by the high priest of the home.

### *Priests That Sin!*

Consider the next verse, "This is why he has to offer sacrifices for his own sins, as well as for the sins of the people" (Heb. 5:3). The priest of the home is also a transgressor of the laws of God. This creates a small dilemma. He is to offer sacrifices for the sins of the people while he is a sinner himself. Every minister in the land can relate to this. God may put a message on our hearts dealing with some type of holiness or consecration, while we know in our own hearts that we haven't fully measured up to the very standard we are preaching.

The high priest is called to offer sacrifices for the sins of others. How do we do that if we are not sinless ourselves? We do it through making sacrifices for ourselves also. This brings us into the area of prayer called confession. The priest's prayer life must contain intercession, which is praying for others, as well as confession. This is to be a daily part of our prayer life. The high priest should be living in a continual state of repentance. It is one thing for us to repent at the time of our salvation, it is another thing for us to live in a continual state of keeping ourselves under God. We should be asking God to search our own hearts on a daily basis. That is what keeps things in right perspective when you consider the sins of others. Realizing that we are nothing more than a forgiven person is what allows us to continue to forgive others.

## An Honorable Office

Hebrews 5:4 says, "No one takes this honor upon himself; he must be called by God, just as Aaron was." The position of the high priest of the home is an honorable office but it is not one that we can boast in. We have been appointed to this position by virtue of being a man. It is not something we have earned. We are to never lord over others as if we did something to deserve this position. No one takes this honor upon himself. There must be humility in the position.

It is only through humility that we can fully fulfill the duties of this position. The position of the high priest is nothing more than a complete dependence upon God. Consider Hebrews 5:5, "So Christ also did not take upon himself the glory of becoming a high priest. But God said to him, 'You are my Son; today I have become your Father.' " Even though Jesus was worthy of the position, He remained humble in the sight of God.

"During the days of Jesus' life on earth, he offered up prayers and petitions with loud cries and tears to the one who could save him from death, and he was heard because of his reverent submission" (Heb. 5:7). God heard the prayers of our High Priest because He was pious which means He feared God or was in submission to God. Jesus did nothing out of disrespect. Everything He did was out of reverence for His Father.

Respect for God is what causes our prayers to be heard. We are to be praying for our families. If anything can quicken the answer to a prayer, it will be our own obedience to God. Even though we may be praying for others, our own obedience to God affects the answer.

## The Suffering Priest

"Although he was a son, he learned obedience from what he suffered" (Heb. 5:8). This verse helps us understand Christ even more. Even though He was the very Son of God, He learned obedience from what He suffered. This is not a reference to the suffering He went through on the Cross, but rather the suffering He went through before the Cross. He stresses His own self-denial.

Consider the description of Christ in Philippians 2:5-8, "Your attitude should be the same as that of Christ Jesus: Who, being in very nature God, did not consider equality with God something to be grasped, but made himself nothing, taking the very nature of a servant, being made in human likeness. And being found in appearance as a man, he humbled himself and became obedient to death — even death on a cross!" If you truly want to function as the high priest of your home, you must have the same attitude as your own High Priest.

# Chapter 7

# *Winning through Losing*

Have you ever considered what was taking place on the Cross? As our Lord hung between heaven and earth, the world and the devil thought they were victorious. As the blood of Christ was being shed, they thought He was finished. As they laid Him in the tomb, wrapped in grave clothes, they thought they would never see Him again.

What a difference three days make! Three days later all the plans of man were destroyed. Three days later the tomb was empty. Three days later the devil was defeated and the plan for the redemption of man was complete. Jesus won by losing.

In Isaiah 53:11 we read, "After the suffering of his soul, he will see the light of life and be satisfied." Even though the suffering of His (Jesus') soul looked like defeat, in reality, His suffering meant our life. Jesus looks back on His suffering and is completely satisfied, knowing that His death has resulted in our life. We win because of His loss. However, because of the love of God for everyone, Jesus sees our new life as His victory. He does not look at his suffering with disdain.

Another way to title this chapter would be, "Life through Death." We have the spiritual life we have today because of the death of our spiritual head, Jesus. If Christ had not died we would not have the means to eternal life that we have today.

## Heads of the Home

Husbands are the priests of the home. They are to be the spiritual heads of their household. They are to lay their lives down for their family in a way similar to how our spiritual head laid His life down for us. The spiritual life of a man's home comes, in large measure, through his self-denial.

Why is it men struggle so much with dying to self? Women don't seem to face the same challenges a man does in this area. When a man is asked to die to something he typically interprets it as losing. Men don't like to be defeated. Men like to be conquerors, they don't like to be conquered. If a man is asked to die to self for the sake of his wife it initially looks as if he is losing and she is winning. The same could have been said of Jesus as He hung on the cross. He gave up His life for His bride. Did that act make Jesus weak or strong?

I once talked with a man who had a very poor relationship with his wife. They never shared any intimacy at all. They seemed to exist together without much trouble, however there had not been any intimate contact for over seven years. As the man would pray about his situation God would tell him to die to it. He would say, "God, I need you to help me in this situation," and all God would say is "Just die to it." The man was confused about just how to die to the situation.

One day in prayer he said, "God, I am willing to die to it, but I don't know how to do that." God spoke to his heart and told him to go to his wife and release her from the guilt he was putting on her because of her lack of desire for him. He said, "But God, if I do that she will never respond to me." That was when he realized that he had not died to the situation at all, he was very much alive and was simply wanting God to change it in his favor. To die to something means you give it up. He was not willing to give it up. He wanted God to bring it to life.

The problem this man was having was that he felt that if he released her from her responsibility in this area of their relationship, she would win and he would lose. This does not sit well with a man's pride. Because of a man's nature he often does not want to be defeated by his wife. He does not want her to win. He wants to conquer her.

Finally, after much prayer, he approached his wife and said, "Honey, I want you to forgive me for putting you under all sorts of pressure to respond to me sexually. I am releasing you from any guilt, I don't want you to feel bad at all for not having any desire for me."

His wife was completely taken by surprise. Her mouth dropped open and she didn't know what to say. A short time later their relationship was completely healed. This situation had been going on for years. For many years this husband could not force his wife into submission. It took God only a couple of weeks to accomplish through humility what pride could not accomplish after several years.

## *Our Example*

Jesus Christ is once again our perfect example for how to live. "To this you were called, because Christ suffered for you, leaving you an example, that you should follow in his steps" (1 Pet. 2:21). Peter is talking about how Jesus failed to defend himself in the midst of injustice. "When they hurled their insults at him, he did not retaliate; when he suffered, he made no threats. Instead, he entrusted himself to him who judges justly" (1 Pet. 2:23). Entrusting yourself to God is simply believing that God is who He says He is. If God says that vengeance is His we must believe Him. "For we know him who said, "It is mine to avenge; I will repay" (Heb. 10:30). To entrust yourself to God is to humble yourself, believing that God will care for you in the midst of injustice.

I had a friend who learned about entrusting himself to God to the greatest degree anybody could. He developed an inoperable brain tumor. The doctors had done all they could. His family and church had prayed all they could and he was dying. After suffering for over two years with his condition fluctuating from fair to bad to fair, he was worn out. In a conversation with another friend of mine he said, "I just want to go to heaven."

My friend said, "What about your family?" (He was a husband and father of three small children.)

He said, "In my suffering and praying and reading the Bible I have come to believe that heaven is everything God says it is. I just want to go to heaven."

My bewildered friend said, "But you have three small children. Don't you want to stay and care for them?"

His only answer was, "I have come to believe that God is everything that He says He is. If God is calling me to heaven then I must entrust my children to Him. He is quite capable of caring for them even in ways I would never have imagined. I completely trust Him."

A few months later, he died, but he learned a great lesson while on earth. God can be trusted even in death. My friend displayed a level of faith that I wish I had. His faith allowed him to entrust even his children and wife to God. He may have lost his physical life, but I believe he has won a much more important battle. He has left a legacy of faith for his wife and children. That legacy will go with them all their days.

## *In the Same Way*

It is in the context of bringing yourself under the one in authority over you that we read the following verse: "Wives, *in the same way* be submissive to your husbands so that, if any of them do not believe the word, they may be won over without words by the behavior of their wives" (1 Pet. 3:1). The key phrase here is, "in the same way." Peter is telling women that they should be in submission in the same way that Christ was. Peter then goes into detail on how a woman can win her husband to Christ through her Christlikeness.

First Peter 3:7 then addresses husbands in a similar manner: "Husbands, *in the same way* be considerate as you live with your wives, and treat them with respect as the weaker partner and as heirs with you of the gracious gift of life, so that nothing will hinder your prayers." This verse starts off with the same phrase, "in the same way." This does not mean that husbands are to submit to their wives, but rather that they are to live in submission to their head the way Christ lives in submission to His head, the Father.

Should a man submit to his wife? That question can be answered by asking another. Did Christ submit to the Church? To both of these the answer is "no." Everyone of us are asked to submit to our heads. Christ submitted to His head, the Father. Husbands are to submit to their head, Jesus. Christ's humility allowed Him to follow the leading of His Father even to the point of dying for those that were weaker than Him. This is the essence of Philippians 2:8: "And being found in appearance as a man, he humbled himself and became obedient to death — even death on a cross!"

God the Father wants you and I to become heirs of the gracious gift of life. The only way that is possible is through the death of His Son.

Today, husbands are called to submit to Jesus, their head, and be considerate of their wives as the weaker vessel because they, too, are heirs of the gracious gift of life. It's not that the salvation of a man's family comes through his self-denial, the way ours came through Christ's, it's that his denial of self reveals his submission to Christ. The revelation of Christ to his family is what leads them to Christ. It's the very same thing Peter was teaching to the women. A husband's salvation does not come through his wife's submission to Christ. However, if she will submit to Christ she will reveal Him to her husband in a way that will win him over.

If a man will lay down his life for his family he is winning the salvation of his children and he is winning the undying love of his wife. He wins through his death-to-self.

## The Weaker Vessel

I once heard a preacher talking about the woman as the weaker vessel. He stated that this does not make the woman an inferior vessel. This is strictly related to physical strength. He went on to say the woman is like a beautiful crystal vase that glimmers and sparkles in the sunlight. Though it is very beautiful, it is also very delicate and needs to be treated with care. The man, on the other hand, is like a hundred pound clay pot. The clay pot is certainly stronger, but not in the least superior. Because of a man's physical nature, being the stronger of the two, society pressures him into being the leader in a way that is contrary to the nature of Christ. Christ's way is submission, not force.

Christ submitted to His father because we are the weaker vessel (mankind). He could have come to earth and used His mighty power and strength to force us into submission. However, that would have crushed our spirit and made us nothing more than puppets. Christ wants our willful submission to Him, just as a husband wants the willful submission of his wife. Therefore, He set the example we should follow by willfully submitting to His superior.

## Powerful Prayers

First Peter 3:7 says that our submission to God and the proper treatment of our wives is what makes our prayers powerful. A man's prayers are made powerful through a simple principle called "life through death." The humble man truly believes that other people are better than him. Through humility you place others over yourself. When you die for the sake of another you are in essence saying, "God I don't deserve to live as much as they do. I want you to give them the desires of their heart."

This identifies the heart of the whole issue. Our unregenerate nature says that we are better than them. Our new Christ-like nature says they are better than us. The reason a man's prayers are hindered when he does not treat his wife with respect is that the lack of respect comes from a heart that is seeking to exalt itself above others. This is completely contrary to the heart of Jesus. Jesus did not even consider equality with God as something He should seek after. Instead he humbled himself. He brought himself under His father which resulted in the most powerful prayer there ever has been: Father forgive them.

God says that the husband and the wife are both partakers of the precious gift of life. That puts us on an equal basis as far as our redemption is concerned. A man is not greater than a woman. Both are simply recipients of something they do not deserve. When a man mistreats his wife he is saying in essence that he is better in God's eyes than she is. How is that man going to come before the Father in prayer and expect God to even hear him?

What would have happened to us if Jesus, the one who had access to 10,000 angels and all the power of heaven, would not have treated us as the weaker vessel? The word of God is full of paradoxes. One such paradox is that we gain life through death. Another is that the only way to keep your life is to give it away. What Jesus teaches us in His death is that the only way for the stronger to protect the weaker is to die for it. We may want to ask, "How is it that we are protected if our protector dies?" Actually it's quite simple. Through the death of the stronger one he entrusts the weaker to God the father. There is no protection outside of the Father. Outside of the protection of the Father there is only wrath, death, and destruction.

### Protection

Dad, do you want to protect your family? Then die to self and give yourself to prayer so that God can become the protector of your home. For over 15 years I have traveled full-time teaching prayer seminars. It has not always been an easy thing to leave my family and go on the road. When I first started out I would pray constantly for God to protect my wife and son. After some time God began to deal with me about my lack of faith. I was under the impression that praying for them the way I did was a sign of faith and then God showed me that it was actually the opposite.

As God was dealing with me about my lack of faith concerning the protection of my family this verse came alive to me. "The angel of the Lord encamps around those who fear him, and he delivers them" (Ps. 34:7). What God was saying to me was that unless I lived in fear of Him there was really no use in praying for His protection. God's angel encamps around those who fear Him. It's automatic, it's not something I need to conjure up. I don't need to pray over and over for God to protect my family. I need to humble myself and bring myself before my Father each day. I need to develop a lifestyle of seeking God. That is some of what it is to live in fear (respect) of God.

The word "encamp" literally means to pitch a tent. The angel of the Lord pitches a tent and takes up residence at the home of those who fear the Lord. When the angel of the Lord is present we need not live in fear. I remember hearing the testimony of a former Satanist. She was talking about all sorts of things that the average person cannot really relate to. She was practicing her witchcraft on many people and finding that she was basically unstoppable. The thing that finally brought her to Christ was that of seeing a 12-foot angel.

She had tapped into a spirit realm where she found all sorts of power. She believed that nothing could stop her. Men and women were being manipulated left and right. One day a group of Satanists was going to the home of a Christian because this man was opposing what they were doing. They intended to do him harm. In the middle of the night they showed up at his house with the intention of breaking in. As they approached his home they were all stopped in their tracks as they gazed upon a 12-foot angel with a sword in his hand. They could not move! They just stood there in complete amazement. After some time the angel told them to move on and they did. This was the first time this Satanist ever encountered something more powerful than herself. It eventually led her to accept Christ as her Saviour.

The man in the house had no idea that the Satanists were coming to do him harm. While he was asleep the angel of the Lord, who had pitched a tent in his yard, was on guard. The man slept in a calm assurance that God was his protector. Through his own denial of self he offered more protection than he could ever have offered in his own strength.

## Dying to Self

Prayer is considered one of the most effective ways to die to self. Consider Matthew 6:5-6: "And when you pray, do not be like the hypocrites, for they love to pray standing in the synagogues and on the street corners to be seen by men. I tell you the truth, they have received their reward in full. But when you pray, go into your room, close the door and pray to your Father, who is unseen. Then your Father, who sees what is done in secret, will reward you." In this setting Jesus is countering the Pharisees who love to be seen as spiritual. He tells us to enter into a prayer closet. It's not that a person cannot pray in other places, it's that Jesus was trying to point out the haughty spirit of the Pharisees.

Hypocrites never pray in secret. They love to be seen. The only ones who will pray in secret are those who will give up a position of exaltation among men. Why is secret prayer so hard to find? It's because men love to be seen especially when they are doing something spiritual. When we are seen praying or doing anything spiritual it exalts us. Public prayer may be quite in order from time to time. When the pastor calls for a prayer meeting there certainly is nothing wrong with coming to the church and praying with other people. In public prayer you do very little confessing of sin. You primarily pray for others.

In private prayer you bring yourself before God in a very intimate way. When I enter into the closet of prayer it's just God and me. I open my heart and He does surgery. Private prayer is becoming more and more difficult to find today because of the haughtiness of men. Private prayer humbles us. It brings us before the One who knows all things. It brings us to a place of death. However, life comes through that death. The more a man will humble himself the more his family experiences the presence of God.

## *Good for Evil*

When we get our eyes fixed on Jesus and follow Him as our example in all things, we cannot get away from the Cross. At the Cross our Saviour was repaying good for evil. The nature of man is to repay evil for evil. The nature of Christ is to do just the opposite. Peter continues in this chapter to challenge us in the same way, "Do not repay evil with evil or insult with insult, but with blessing, because to this you were called so that you may inherit a blessing" (1 Pet. 3:9).

If someone does something we would consider evil to us we are to die to what our unregenerate nature would like to do. "He must turn from evil [the unregenerate nature] and do good [follow Christ's nature]; he must seek peace and pursue it" (1 Pet. 3:11). Leadership is not always getting what you want. Leadership is setting the example you want others to follow. In that sense leadership requires a death. We must die to our own ego. We must die to the desire to be the King of men. The Bible does indicate that one day we will reign with Christ (Rev. 20:6), however the emphasis is on "reigning with Christ." To reign with Christ you become a servant of men — you do not look for men to serve you.

First Peter 3:14 is the acid test in determining whether or not a man is Christlike or not: "But even if you should suffer for what is right, you are blessed." This is what tests our motives. Some men may have already thought this principle through and said to themselves, "All I have to do is give up my rights and then God will turn my situation around so that I ultimately get what I want." WRONG! What God is calling men to is that of Christlikeness. Will we be content doing the right thing even if it never works to our benefit?

Suppose a man were to return good for someone else's evil and the whole thing backfires. Suppose those you do good to never repent of their evil. Will you still do good? Jesus would and does. Jesus would have died for us even if no one would have ever accepted Him as their Lord. He would have done it because He came to do the will of His father. We can do no less for our families.

# Chapter 8

# Preparing the Heart for Prayer

The whole secret to becoming a man of God lies in prayer. "The Lord confides in those who fear him; he makes his covenant known to them" (Ps. 25:14). This verse tells us that the Lord reveals His secrets to those who fear Him. To fear God is to hold Him in reverence. To reverence God is to honor Him with your time.

Have you ever considered why Jesus prayed so much? I used to ask God that question all the time. I thought that if anyone had the Father figured out, Jesus did. One day, the Lord simply spoke to my heart and said, "Jesus didn't pray in order to figure me out. Jesus prayed because He had me figured out." Then it hit me, Jesus prayed out of a respect for who He knew the Father to be. In light of who Jesus knew the Father to be, it would have been quite disrespectful not to honor Him with His time.

Prayer is the active practice of fearing the Lord. "The Lord confides in those who fear him." In other words, the Lord reveals the secrets of the kingdom of God to those who respect Him enough to give Him the time He deserves.

## Heart Surgery

When it comes to developing a heart for prayer, a heart that seriously respects God, there is some significant heart surgery a person must go through. The heart is the key to a life of drawing close to God. If a person is not willing to allow God to develop his heart into a heart that wants Him, then it will be very difficult to remain consistent in the life of prayer. Without a deep prayer life, it is virtually impossible to become anything more than religious.

"I will give them a heart to know me, that I am the Lord. They will be my people, and I will be their God, for they will return to me with all their heart" (Jer. 24:7). God wants each of us to have a heart that knows Him. In order to gain that type of heart we must do away with the stony heart we now have. "I will give them an undivided heart and put a new spirit in them; I will remove from them their heart of stone and give them a heart of flesh" (Ezek. 11:19). A heart of stone has no life in it. A heart of stone is a hard heart. Pharaoh had a heart of stone.

In Exodus 4:21 we read, "The Lord said to Moses, 'When you return to Egypt, see that you perform before Pharaoh all the wonders I have given you the power to do. But I will harden his heart so that he will not let the people go.' " Without understanding all that God was doing here, we might think it was unfair for Him to harden Pharaoh's heart. Actually this simply verifies why it is so important to allow God to work in our hearts. As Moses was trying to free the Hebrew children from the grip of Egypt, Pharaoh had three different opportunities to allow God to give him a heart of flesh, but in each instance he refused. Rebellion is the ingredient in the heart that causes it to harden. Pharaoh had rebellion in his heart long before God ever dealt with him.

I have heard it described this way. If you take a pound of clay and a pound of butter and set them both outside under a blazing sun, one will melt and the other will harden. They have two different reactions because of what they were made up of long before the sun shone upon them. The sun treated them the same, but there were two different reactions. When the Scriptures say that God hardened Pharaoh's heart, it doesn't necessarily mean that God set it up so that Pharaoh could not have repented even if he had wanted to. It simply means that when God dealt with him, when God shone His light upon him, his heart hardened because of what was in it long before God ever dealt with him. Consider this: God dealt with Moses also, but his heart melted. "Glancing this way and that and seeing no one, he killed the Egyptian and hid him in the sand" (Exod. 2:12). God sent Moses into the desert for 40 years because of his sin, and yet Moses came out of that experience as a man of God with a heart of flesh. The only way God can remove the stony heart is through allowing Him to do some heart surgery on us.

A heart of flesh is a live, beating, breathing, heart. It is a heart that is filled with the spirit of God. A heart of flesh finds its life in the presence of God. It pants for the presence of God. It pursues the presence of God. A heart of flesh is pliable. It conforms, it reforms, and it transforms. I once saw on a church sign, "Blessed are the flexible, for they shall not be bent out of shape." A heart of flesh is a flexible heart. When it encounters the unchangeable laws of God, it accommodates them.

## King Hezekiah

We can learn much from the heart of King Hezekiah. "Hezekiah was twenty-five years old when he became king, and he reigned in Jerusalem twenty-nine years. His mother's name was Abijah daughter of Zechariah. He did what was right in the eyes of the Lord, just as his father David had done" (2 Chron. 29:1-2). Hezekiah did what was right in the eyes of the Lord. That is the kind of thing any man would want to have said about him. What made Hezekiah different from many of the kings who preceded him? His heart! Hezekiah had a heart to know God.

## Open the Door

Consider one of his first official acts as king. In 2 Chronicles 29:3 we read, "In the first month of the first year of his reign, he opened the doors of the temple of the Lord and repaired them." Hezekiah opened the doors of the temple of the Lord. Today we are the temple of the Lord. The doorway into our temple is the heart. If God is going to dwell in a man, He does so through entering into the heart and He enters through confession.

I was a Christian many years before I began to pray. I did have a form of prayer in my life prior to that, but I had no real pursuit of God. I refer to it as a "typical Christian-type prayer life." I prayed on Sundays because everybody prays on Sunday, or I prayed if someone asked me to pray, but that was about it. I was content just believing that I was a Christian and that when I die I will go to heaven. Through a number of circumstances in my life, I began to understand my need to spend more time with the Lord. God began to change me as I spent time in His presence. Those changes were very drastic. In fact, prayer changed my Christian life just as drastically as Christ originally changed my life.

When I began to give myself over to a life of prayer I often prayed Psalms 139:23-24: "Search me, O God, and know my heart." I would ask God over and over to search me and know my heart. Asking God to search our own hearts is not for God's sake, it's for our sake. Consider Proverbs 27:19. "As water reflects a face, so a man's heart reflects the man." God knows our heart long before we even open it to Him. The heart is simply a revelation of who a man really is.

It is important for all of us to come to this place of asking God to reveal to us what's in our hearts. It seems that some men are afraid of opening themselves up to God that way. Have you ever asked yourself why it is difficult to confess sin? Why are we afraid to open our hearts to God? Do we think we are going to shock God with some little tidbit that He doesn't already know about us? Suppose one day you are in prayer and you decide to tell God something about yourself. You say something like, "God, there's something I haven't told you, but I have a terrible temper."

Do you think God is going to say, "Wow, I didn't know that! You shouldn't have told me! Don't you know that I am God?" We will never astound God with any revelation of who we are. God already knows who we are.

It is not for God's sake that we reveal and confess these things, it's for us. It's very similar to the situation you find with alcoholics. You really cannot help them until they admit they are alcoholics. Until they admit that, they will refuse help because to accept help would be to admit to the problem. "Search me, O God, and know my heart," becomes a very important prayer in preparing a heart that knows God. If God is going to find a comfortable dwelling place within our hearts, we must be willing to deal with those things that make Him uncomfortable. This addresses the issue of confession. Confessing our sin is the most freeing thing we can do.

A regular practice of confessing your sin to God can keep you on a right path. I believe in keeping a "short account" with God. What I mean by that is this; deal with your sin right away. Never let a sin become so big or unattended to in your life that the only way to deal with it is through some major adjustment or public confession in your life. If a person would daily bring his heart before God and say something like, "Lord, show me the things that are in my heart that are not pleasing to you." If you will do that, then you can deal with it in a personal, private manner. If a person will allow God to stop a sin in its tracks, through confession, he can save himself great embarrassment.

## Repairing the Heart

The final part of 2 Chronicles 29:3 says, ". . . and repaired them." After Hezekiah opened the doors to the temple he repaired them. This deals with forgiveness. The doors to the temple had fallen into disrepair. They were not even usable. If the door to our heart is broken, it must be repaired. First we ask God to inspect our hearts by praying, "Search me, God." As God begins to bring to light the things that are in our hearts that are displeasing to Him, we take care of it or repair it through asking for forgiveness. After confession is forgiveness. Let's continue to integrate 2 Chronicles 29:3 into Psalm 139:23. After David prays "Search me, O God," he prays, "Test me and know my anxious thoughts" (Ps. 139:23). God will test us to see if we are serious about asking for forgiveness. Remember Proverbs 27:19 said that the heart actually reflects what a man is. When we ask God to forgive us, we prove our desire to be forgiven by being tested. David prayed, "Test me!" This reflected what was really in David's heart. He said in essence, "Lord, just to prove my desire to be what you want me to be, test me."

"Test me and know my anxious thoughts." The word "thoughts" in this verse means "desires." The idea behind this is that anything that is really a desire of our heart, will occupy our thoughts. So David is saying in essence, "Test me by examining what actually occupies my thoughts."

The proof that we truly want to be set free from those things that bind us, is that we give our thoughts over to the things of God. Paul teaches us something similar to this in Romans 12:2: "Do not conform any longer to the pattern of this world, *but be transformed by the renewing of your mind.* Then you will be able to test and approve what God's will is — his good, pleasing, and perfect will." God must occupy our thoughts. If God does not occupy them, if we are still giving our thoughts over to the sin that besets us, then we are not serious in our desire to be set free — thus, we fail the test. We will not be transformed and our confession is not true.

The pursuit of God should be the primary desire of our heart. When I first began to pray, I would often say, "God, I want you. I just want you."

God would then put me to the test and say, "Are you willing to forsake everything that stands as a hindrance in your relationship with me?"

I was saying, "God, I want you," and because of that, God was revealing what was really in my heart. I said, "God, I want you," and He said, "Then why are your thoughts occupied with things other than me?" He said, "If you are really serious about your confession of sin, it will be reflected in what you give your thoughts to."

Keep in mind that we are trying to repair the heart. The only reason God reveals things about us that are displeasing to Him is for the purpose of reconciliation. God wants us to draw near to Him. It is not a negative thing at all for God to show us the deceit of our hearts. God wants to put the things we call desires to the test to reveal the true nature of our hearts to us.

"Out of the overflow of the heart the mouth speaks" (Matt. 12:34). If we tell God that we desire, want, and need Him, and then refuse to spend time in His presence and time in His Word, it reveals that there is still deceit in our hearts, and our mouth has just revealed it. This is why it is so important for us to allow God to search our hearts. We really do not know what our hearts are made up of until we allow God to reveal it to us. Once God has revealed our hearts, we need to then ask God to forgive us of whatever stands between Him and us.

I had a friend who once spent several hours in the presence of God simply allowing Him to overhaul his heart. He said he sat in the middle of his living room floor after his family had gone to sleep and simply opened his heart to the Lord. First he took the Word of God out and began to read. He didn't really have an agenda. He wasn't looking for God to speak anything in particular to him, he was simply opening himself to whatever God wanted to say to him through His Word.

After spending considerable time in the Word and presence of God, he began to confess everything that came to his mind. He was not in any particular rush here either. He simply said, "God, I want you to show me my heart." It was not a troublesome thing at all, it was a cleansing thing. He spent much time praising, weeping, and confessing. However, he said it was one of the most beautiful experiences he has ever had. He was well on his way to developing a heart to know God.

## Restoring the Heart

Consider the next thing Hezekiah did. "He brought in the priests and the Levites, assembled them in the square on the east side and said: "Listen to me, Levites! Consecrate yourselves now and consecrate the temple of the Lord, the God of your fathers. Remove all defilement from the sanctuary" (2 Chron. 29:4-5). Removing all the defilement deals with repentance. If we are to develop a true heart for God, we must first confess all sin, then we ask God to forgive us, and finally we must repent.

It is one thing to ask for forgiveness, it is another thing to turn from sin. One of the reasons we find that we are confessing the same sin over and over is because we are quicker at confessing than we are at repenting. To remove the defilement means we must change the path of life we are on. If we bring in Psalms 139:24 we will understand this better. "See if there is any offensive way in me, and lead me in the way everlasting." What is an offensive way? It's any "way" that does not lead us closer to God. The way the priests removed the defilement from the temple was through confessing the sins, or the way of life, of their forefathers.

"Our fathers were unfaithful; they did evil in the eyes of the Lord our God and forsook him. They turned their faces away from the Lord's dwelling place and turned their backs on him. This is why our fathers have fallen by the sword and why our sons and daughters and our wives are in captivity" (2 Chron. 29:6-9). The "way" of their hearts was determined by the sins of their fathers. God was asking them to change their ways. He was asking them to repent.

There is great hope for those who repent. Even though the sins of the fathers are passed down to even the third generation, there is still hope. "You shall not bow down to them or worship them; for I, the Lord your God, am a jealous God, punishing the children for the sin of the fathers to the third and fourth generation of those who hate me" (Exod. 20:5). Those who hate the Lord are represented by those who won't repent from their sins. If, however, a person repents, he can be freed from the effects of his father's sin. Consider Ezekiel 18:17. "He withholds his hand from sin and takes no usury or excessive interest. He keeps my laws and follows my decrees. He will not die for his father's sin; he will surely live."

The person who repents changes his way of life. He

no longer does things the way it's always been done. It's almost as if we make Jesus our Saviour by asking Him to forgive us of our sin, but we make Him our Lord by repenting of our sin. One of the mistakes of today's Church is that we teach more about the benefits of the resurrection than we do about the lordship of Christ. We try to draw people to Christ by highlighting all the benefits that are ours as children of God. If we fail to balance that with His lordship, we create a false image of what it really means to be a Christian.

Stressing the lordship of Christ will bring us into living in a continual state of repentance. Certainly, we repent in order to originally come to Christ. However, after that initial time of repentance, we are to live in a continual state of repentance. A continual state of repentance is what keeps our hearts pure. Repentance is much like submission or patience. These words have to do with bringing yourself under God. In order for Jesus to be the Lord of our lives, He is to live "above" us. He is to direct our every thought. "We take captive every thought to make it obedient to Christ" (2 Cor. 10:5). He is to direct our every step. "Whoever claims to live in him must walk as Jesus did" (1 John 2:6). To live in a spirit of repentance means living beneath the Lord to the point that others really do not see you when they look at your life; they see Jesus only.

Preparing your heart for prayer can be summed up in one word: surrender. Surrender your heart to Christ. Give Him your will. Give Him your plans. Give Him your talents. Give Him your heart. If you get into a battle with God, you will ultimately lose. You may be able to live today without God, but you can't live forever without God.

# PART THREE

# Soldout Souls

# Chapter 9

# The Value of a Soul

America needs men with sold-out souls. It needs men who see service to God as the priority of their lives. When children seek God, He smiles on the nation. When women seek God, He nurtures a nation. When men seek God, He revives a nation. Men are, by nature, leaders. When they allow God to lead them they in turn lead others. God, give us men with sold-out souls!

Have you ever considered the value of your soul? In Mark 8:36 we read, "What good is it for a man to gain the whole world, yet forfeit his soul?" God tells us that a soul is worth more than the whole world. He says that even if we gained all the riches of the world and lost our souls, we would have nothing.

First Thessalonians 5:23 says, "May your whole *spirit, soul* and *body* be kept blameless at the coming of our Lord Jesus Christ." The Scriptures teach us that man is made up of three basic parts — body, soul, and spirit. The body is simply flesh and bones. It counts for nothing. If you remove the soul and spirit from a man you would have nothing left but bones! John 6:63 says, "The Spirit gives life; the flesh counts for nothing. The words I have spoken to you are spirit and they are life."

The spirit is the life of God within you. It really has very little to do with you. God puts it there when you surrender your life to Him. In that sense, you do not control it or have much to do with it at all. Ephesians 4:30 does indicate that we can grieve the Holy Spirit: "And do not grieve the Holy Spirit of God, with whom you were sealed for the day of redemption." The spirit is the life of God within you.

The soul, however, differs from these other items. The soul is your humanness. Matthew 10:39 gives us one example, "Whoever finds his life will lose it, and whoever loses his life for my sake will find it." The word "life" in this verse is the Greek word, *psuche,* which means soul. It is your human nature. Your soul is the very thing you love the most about yourself. It really is the essence of who you are. That is why this verse tells us that if we put ourselves above God (love our own life more than we love God) we will actually lose our life, or soul.

The soul is the only thing about you that can be redeemed. That is why it is so important and valuable to God. Your soul is eternal. It lives forever. It will either live forever with God or forever without God. There is nothing more important to God than that which he created to live forever.

The Bible says that if you would love your neighbor the way you love yourself, you could fulfill the whole law. In our humanness, we don't love anything the way we love ourselves. Most everything we do is for self. Therefore, if we would love others the way we love ourselves, we would die for them. We would treat them with great respect. We would go the second mile for them. We would turn the other cheek for them. We would fulfill the entire law which is exactly what Jesus did for us.

## Our Will

Our soul is where our will lives. When we surrender our will, we surrender our soul. However, God will not violate our free will. If He were to violate our free will, He would be going against the whole nature of a relationship. The beauty of a relationship is the free will or the freedom to choose. The beauty of my wife's relationship with me is that she has the freedom to leave me, but chooses to stay with me. If she had no will and had to stay with me even though she wanted to leave, where would the beauty be in that?

If I were a manipulator and controlled my wife to the point that she had no choice but to stay with me, even though she wanted to leave, where would the beauty of our relationship be? When we surrender our soul to God, we are surrendering our will also. We are saying, "God, I want to be with you forever." That's beautiful! The Bible indicates that those who ultimately go to heaven are those who truly wanted and chose God.

Freedom of choice really describes the beauty of the prayer life also. The act of prayer is that of surrendering the will to God. God will not force us to pray. There must be a desire for God before you will come into submission to Him. The word "submission" in the Greek means to put yourself under something or someone. It has a meaning similar to the words patience or perseverance.

Consider what James teaches us in 1:1-3: "James a servant of God and of the Lord Jesus Christ, To the twelve tribes scattered among the nations: Greetings. Consider it pure joy, my brothers, whenever you face trials of many kinds, because you know that the testing of your faith develops perseverance." He says to consider it joy when we face tests, because tests reveal to us how much we live in submission to God. James is teaching us that temptation is a challenge to come up above or to come out from under God. Satan does not want us living under God. Therefore any temptation, regardless of how it comes, is always a challenge to do your own thing.

Whenever a man is faced with temptation he is also faced with a decision concerning the lordship of Christ in his life. It really does not matter in what form the temptation comes. It is always Satan's challenge to no longer live under Christ. When we live "under," Christ is over us. Christ being over us denotes His lordship in our lives. Satan does not want Jesus to be Lord of our lives, so he tempts us. When we make a decision concerning our temptation, our decision is determined by the lordship of our life. If we obey Christ it's because Jesus lords over us. If we give into the temptation it's because we have placed ourselves over Christ. Someone once said, "Jesus is not Lord of some of your life. He is either Lord of all or not at all."

## Surrendering the Will

The prayer life is a daily surrendering of the will to God. It is the practice of bringing yourself under God. It is a daily dying to self. It's giving him complete control of your soul. It's a beautiful thing to live in submission to God. Unfortunately, I believe that we often think of submission as self-discipline. Many times the first thing we think of when we hear something about dying to self is that it's really nothing more than self-discipline. Self-discipline can differ completely from self-denial. It is entirely possible to deny self for the purpose of self-gratification. Physical exercise falls under this category. People often exercise for personal benefit. That really is not self-denial, it's self-discipline.

Self-denial is that of denying yourself a position of exaltation among men. It is common to look at the self-discipline of Christ, and try to practice it thinking that that is all there is to being Christ-like. We see Him praying and fasting, so we try to pray and fast like Him. There is certainly nothing wrong with the practice of either of those things, but those things fall more under the category of self-discipline than anything else.

The one practice of Christ that most people reject is His self-denial. He did not allow the people to exalt Him. He did not want His miracles published - we do! He did not want those who were healed to do anything but worship God - we want them to tell everyone what we did!

Often it's because of self-discipline (the practice of prayer and fasting) that miracles and the movement of the Spirit happens. However, at that point we are to exercise self-denial. It is not uncommon to see people practicing the same self-discipline Christ did so that through the subsequent miracles that follow those practices they can gain self-glory and esteem among men. There is very little self-denial in that.

## God Never Gives Up

Because of what our soul means to God, He will never give up on getting us to surrender to Him. This applies to both the believer and the non-believer. Look at what Job 33:28-30 says. "He redeemed my soul from going down to the pit, and I will live to enjoy the light. God does all these things to a man — twice, even three times — to turn back his soul from the pit, that the light of life may shine on him."

Listen to how the KJV puts it. "He will deliver his soul from going into the pit, and his life shall see the light. Lo, all these things worketh God often times with man, To bring back his soul from the pit, to be enlightened with the light of the living."

God continually works in us to keep our souls from going down into the pit. He wants us to be enlightened with the light of His Son. When we begin to pray for someone, God goes to work. As long as we pray, He continues to work. However, because He will not violate a person's free will, our prayers are not always answered the way we would like them to be. When we pray, the Holy Spirit gains a freedom to arrange a person's circumstances so as to make it easy for them to surrender their will to God.

The person being prayed for is constantly being brought to a point of decision. He finds himself coming face to face with his decision concerning his soul. Every time he turns around, he runs into a Christian. The people he works with are witnessing to him. He hears it on the radio and television. All of this takes place to bring him to a point of decision. If, at the point of decision, he refuses Christ, then the Holy Spirit simply goes back to work to bring him to another point of decision. That process continues as long as we continue to pray for him. As Job put it, "God will do this time and time again, to keep our soul from going down to the pit."

Even men who curse God, who shake their fist in the face of God and challenge him saying, "If there is a God, let him strike me dead," then they walk off laughing, saying, "See, there is no God." Those men fail to realize that the very breath they drew to curse their God was given to them by their God and that God will not strike them dead because He wants to give them another chance to repent. God wants to keep our souls from going down into the pit.

### More Valuable than a Castle

I once had an opportunity to visit an ancient king's castle in Spain. It was the most elegant thing I have ever seen. The artwork alone was worth millions. The structure itself was worth even more than the art. It had 30-some bedrooms, it had dining halls, ball rooms, and bathrooms. To top it all off, it had one of the largest church sanctuaries attached to it I have ever seen. Then we went down to the tomb of the king who built the castle. He was laid to rest with several generations of heirs to his throne. The staircase had marble halls and steps. The railings were brass and gold. The room itself was all gold, brass, and marble.

As I stood there looking at all the glory and glamour of it, I realized that it means nothing compared to the value of a soul. God would pay any price for your soul.

We went from the castle to the tomb of Franco, the former dictator of Spain. This is another amazing structure. It's carved into a mountain-side 300 yards deep. It has a cross on top of it that is 300 yards tall. The money it took to build this monument to man is more than I will ever see. Yet even at that, God would gladly pay it for your soul. The amount is nothing compared to the value God puts on your soul.

## No Amount of Money

God would pay any price to gain your soul. However, there is no dollar figure that could be put on the value of a soul. God demonstrated the fact that He would pay anything for your soul when He gave His only Son to die for you. But there is no dollar amount you can put on the value of a soul because the value of a soul is based on love. You cannot sell what you love. However, you can give it away. God gave His Son. For God so loved that He gave. God did not sell His son; He gave Him. God could never have sold His son because that would have been putting a dollar amount on Him. To sell Him would have been as if God was saying, "My son is worth this much." God gave that which meant the most to Him, His own son.

The value of the soul lies within the very framework of who God is. Why is a child so valuable to his parents? Because that child contains within it the parent's very life. How much would a child be worth? You couldn't put a price on it. In fact you wouldn't even want to put a price on it. Christian parents would possibly pay any price to gain their child, but they would never sell their child. I have heard of people paying millions of dollars in ransom fees to get their kidnapped child back. I have heard of pregnant mothers putting their own lives on the line to give birth to a child, but rarely do you hear of parents selling their child.

I would rather allow my son to die than to sell him. That may sound like an odd statement, but we need to understand a principle here. It is all based on love. God would never have sold His Son, but He allowed him to die. Abraham would never have taken any amount of money for his son Isaac, but he was willing to put him to death for God's sake. He was willing to give him to God.

Consider what the Bible says about love. First Corinthians 13:4-8 says, "Love is patient, love is kind. It does not envy, it does not boast, it is not proud. It is not rude, it is not self-seeking, it is not easily angered, it keeps no record of wrongs. Love does not delight in evil but rejoices with the truth. It always protects, always trusts, always hopes, always perseveres. Love never fails"

Love is not self-seeking. If Abraham would have bartered with God over the value of Isaac's soul and come up with some dollar figure, and then offered to sell Isaac to God, that would have been self-seeking and something less than love. Instead Abraham showed his love for God when he put that which meant the most to him, his son, on the block, and was ready to sacrifice him to God. He was willing to give his son, but he would never have sold him.

God will never put a dollar figure on the value of a soul because He loves us. We have His life within us. He says your soul is worth more than any amount of money. It is worth more than all the riches of this world. It is priceless.

### God's Ultimate Expression

God's ultimate expression of love for us is that He gave us His Son. Our ultimate expression of love back to God, is when we give him our soul. We cannot sell it to Him; that would be self-seeking. We must give it to Him. We must give Him that which means the most to us — because He gave us that which meant the most to Him. Nothing means more to us than ourselves. John 12:25 says, "The man who loves his life will lose it, while the man who hates his life in this world will keep it for eternal life." The Greek word for the word "life" in this verse means soul. So the verse could read, "The man who loves (keeps) his own soul will lose it, while the man who hates (or gives away) his soul will keep it for eternal life."

*To hate our life means to love God more than ourselves.* It means we give ourselves away to God. The idea here is that if we really do love ourselves, then we should love the One who gave us life. The only way to keep our life is to give it back to God.

### The Devoted Soul

In Leviticus 27:28 we read, "'But nothing that a man owns and devotes to the Lord — whether man or animal or family land — may be sold or redeemed; everything so devoted is most holy to the Lord." We are the owners of our souls. When God created us, He gave us souls. It is ours, we own it. However, when we dedicated our life to God, we gave Him our soul. We devoted it to the Lord. We gave up ownership of it. We cannot sell it. If we give our soul to God, He will keep it for us for eternity. If we sell our soul, we lose it.

When something is devoted to the Lord, it becomes holy unto Him. When something is holy it is separated. A holy person lives separated from the world. An ungodly person lives for the world. He will subsequently sell his soul to the world.

First Kings 21:25 says, "There was never a man like Ahab, who sold himself to do evil in the eyes of the Lord." Ahab sold his soul. Selling our soul is equivalent to keeping it for ourselves. Selling our soul is that of giving ourselves over to the sensual pleasures of this life. Selling our soul is nurturing our flesh. It is the opposite of holiness. Holiness is to be separated unto the Lord. Anything devoted unto the Lord is holy. *The only way to keep our life is to give it away to God.* We cannot give God our flesh and bones - they mean nothing to God. We cannot give Him the spirit that dwells within us because that is already His. The only thing we can give Him that is significant is the thing we love the most — our soul, our human nature.

I was once teaching a seminar in a church in Virginia. One day the pastor shared with me an experience he had in prayer. He said he had a practice of telling God how much he loved Him. Over and over in prayer he would say, "Lord I love You."

One day he said, "God, why do I tell You I love You, more than You tell me You love me?" As soon as he asked, he knew it was a stupid question.

God spoke to him and said, "Don't you yet understand the value of your soul? Don't you know that I love you in ways you cannot fully understand? Every blade of grass on every lawn speaks of My love for you. Every leaf on every tree speaks of My love for you. In fact, all of creation screams of My love for you."

The pastor was in awe over this revelation. All day

long he thought about it. The next day in prayer he said, "Thank You, Lord, for showing me how much You love me." As soon as he said that, he knew something was still wrong.

God spoke to him again and said, "I could create a million earths and they would only state My love to a certain point. The fullness of My love for you was expressed in what I allowed My Son to go through just for you. Do you understand what sending My Son to die meant for you?"

He knew he could give a theological answer, but in his heart he knew that he really didn't fully know. So he said, "No."

The Lord said, "To understand that, you would have to understand the Cross. Do you understand that?"

Again the pastor said, "No."

God said, "That's because to understand the cross, you would have to understand Gethsemane. Do you understand that?"

He said, "No."

God replied, "That's because to understand Gethsemane, you would have to understand the cup. Do you understand the cup that My Son drank from?"

By now the Pastor was weeping, and he said, "No."

Then God said, "The cup that Jesus took contains every drop of blood that has ever been shed in all the wars there ever have been and ever will be. It contains all the blood shed in all the murders there ever have been or ever will be. The cup that Jesus took contains every cry of every unwanted child there ever has been or ever will be. Every scream, every hurt of every abused, molested, abandoned child there ever was or ever will be was in there. It contains every tear that has ever been shed over every lost loved one, there ever has been or ever will be. It contains every tear that has ever been shed over every broken marriage there ever has been or ever will be. It contains all the frustrations and heartaches of the alcoholics and drug abusers there ever have been or ever will be. Everything that sin has ever brought into this world or will ever bring into this world was in that cup. That is My love for you. That is the value of your soul. It's expressed in what I was willing to let My Son go through just for you."

The soul is the breath of God, the beauty of man, the wonder of angels, and the envy of devils. It is of an angelic nature, it is a heavenly spark, a heavenly plant, and of a divine offspring. It is a spiritual substance, capable of the knowledge of God, and of union with God, and of communion with God. It is eternal and everlasting.

Our soul, that thing that lies deep within us, is worth more to God than all the riches of this world. And now that we have surrendered it to God, we have said, "God we give You the most important and valuable thing within us, just to show You how much we love You. We love You with all our heart and soul."

# Chapter 10

# *Developing a Seeking Soul*

A sold-out soul not only wants what God wants, it also wants God. It is a soul that is taken up with God. Have you ever wanted God with all your heart and with all your soul? What is it to have a seeking soul? The Bible describes a seeking soul as a soul devoted to God. Consider what 1 Chronicles 22:19 says. "Now devote your heart and soul to seeking the Lord your God. Begin to build the sanctuary of the Lord God, so that you may bring the ark of the covenant of the Lord and the sacred articles belonging to God into the temple that will be built for the Name of the Lord."

First Peter 2:5 teaches us something very similar in regards to building the temple. "You also, like living stones, are being built into a spiritual house to be a holy priesthood, offering spiritual sacrifices acceptable to God through Jesus Christ." The Scriptures indicate that we are being built into a spiritual house. Building is a process. It takes time to devote ourselves wholly to the Lord. It takes commitment, it takes a covenant with Him.

Our opening verse said that God wants us to build the sanctuary of the Lord so that the ark of the covenant can have a place to reside (1 Chron. 22:19). In the Old Testament, the ark was where the presence of God lodged. One of the most important things to the Jewish people was that of having the presence of God in their midst. They knew that when God was with them, they were a blessed people. They knew they were a protected people. They knew they were a cared-for people.

Today we are to build a sanctuary for the Lord, also. However, that sanctuary is ourselves. God lives within us. So King David says in essence, "Now devote your heart and soul to seeking the Lord your God so that you can build the sanctuary of the Lord God." God's dwelling place must be free of self. It must be a place set apart from this world and the spirit of this world.

## Two Types of Cleansing

Devote your heart and soul to seeking the Lord your God. Do you understand what it means to devote your soul to God? A soul is not fully devoted until it is cleansed. However, you cannot cleanse your soul. *God must.* Dr. Gordon Anderson says there are two different types of cleansing rituals in the Bible: (1) things that we can clean, and (2) things that we cannot clean. Things that we can clean are cleaned by water or by blood. Naaman had to wash seven times (2 Kings 5:10). There are many instances of shedding the blood of animals and so forth.

Things that we cannot clean are cleaned by fire. The burnt offerings, burning the clothing of the lepers, and things like that are represented here. We have a choice in the matter. We can be cleansed by the washing of the water of the Word, allowing the Word of God to change our lives, or we can wait until the fire of judgment touches our lives. In either case, the cleansing brings us to a place of devotion.

Dr. Anderson says, "Often, when we think of having devotions, we think of something light or easy. We think it means having a nice quiet time with God where we sit down and read the Bible for a little while and then have some virtuous thoughts of God, then maybe we pray for 10 minutes. However, the true meaning of the word 'devotion' has to do with burning. The word 'devote' really comes from the Latin word 'votive.' You can still purchase votive candles today. They are burned in many Orthodox or Catholic religious practices. They are symbolic of something being burned up and consumed. This is the picture of something devoted to God which is being cleansed by burning. This is the idea behind Hebrews 12:29: 'for our "God is a consuming fire.' "[1]

God wants to consume us so that there is nothing of our flesh left. Then, when we are empty of self, when our soul is devoted to God, we can begin to build the sanctuary of the Lord. It is to be a holy place, separated from this world. To be devoted to God or to have devotions is much more involved than something light and easy - it consumes you. To have a devoted soul, you are to be constantly burning away the love of self or the spirit of this world from your life.

## Burning Away the Fleshly Nature

Leviticus 3:9 says, "From the fellowship offering he is to bring a sacrifice made to the Lord by fire: its fat, the entire fat tail cut off close to the backbone, all the fat that covers the inner parts or is connected to them." Now consider Leviticus 3:16: "The priest shall burn them on the altar as food, an offering made by fire, a pleasing aroma. All the fat is the Lord's." The fat represents your fleshly nature. It represents the unregenerate soul of man. There is no way to clean the soul of its fleshiness without fire. It must be burned away.

The burning comes through the practice of the three

Christian disciplines found in Matthew 6 — giving, praying, and fasting. The practice of these three things develops the life of holiness or devotion. When Jesus talks about these disciplines He encourages us to practice them in private. I believe the reason for that is the humility it takes to do things in private. The proud man does things to be seen of men. He cannot bring himself into the closet of privacy where he stands face to face with his God because that would ultimately destroy his plan for greatness. When he does give, pray, or fast it is with a lot of fanfare. There is no burning or devotion when you gain glory from men.

We are the sanctuary of the Lord. God lives within us. When we are full of self, God has no place to reside. Some seem to believe that since they went through the act of asking Christ into their lives, they no longer need to separate themselves from worldliness because their sins have been forgiven. They view separation from the world as legalism. But Paul said, "I die every day" (1 Cor. 15:31).

There is still a great need for daily devotions. Once we are devoted to God, his freedom within us increases. God's living space within us increases through repentance. It's when we repent of our sin that we die to it. That death creates a holy dwelling place for God. The repentance I'm referring to is a repentance that goes beyond the initial repentance of sin we went through when we were saved. This deals more with living in a state of repentance.

Rex Andrews once said, "The very same state of heart that you were in when you first repented is the state of heart that God wants you to be in when you come before the throne of glory. It is just the same state of heart, exactly, that He wants you to remain in. That is to be your form. It is to be what you really are at the root of your being — lowliness." When we came to Christ we were empty. We had nothing to offer Him at all. We were nothing. Because of that emptiness, Christ can dwell within us. However, if we come out of that state or frame of mind, we become haughty, which is the opposite of lowliness. We then begin to fill God's dwelling place with ourselves.

## Holiness

When something is set apart from this world, specifically for the purpose of drawing closer to God, it becomes holy. Holiness means separation from the world. But holiness is more than just not doing certain worldly things. It has to do with a cutting away of fleshly desires. It's doing things the opposite of how this world does things. Holiness comes through devotion. It comes through burning away the carnal man.

When your soul is devoted to seeking God, you develop a holy place within you for God to dwell. However, we often think of holiness as something that we can strap on from the outside. Holiness is not attained through outward actions. We do not gain holiness by how much we go to church or even by how much we refrain from doing worldly things. You cannot put holiness on - hoping it will work itself inside. Holiness is in you, in the form of Christ, trying to manifest itself through outward actions. You don't become holy through your actions. However, if you are holy it will affect your actions.

## Salvation by Works?

How is a man saved? Is he saved by works? No! Ephesians 2:8-9 teaches us, "For it is by grace you have been saved, through faith — and this not from yourselves, it is the gift of God — not by works, so that no one can boast."

I once heard Dr. Gordon Anderson say, "Suppose

you draw an imaginary line about eye level. Above that line is salvation, below is death. How do we cross that line? If we do only good works the best we could do is bump up against the line's bottom side. The only way to cross the line is through faith. For it is by grace you have been saved, through faith." The Greek word for "faith" is *pistis*. Through *pistis* we cross over to the side of salvation.

Our problem is that we teach that you are saved by faith and then unsaved by works. If you could not cross the line through good works, you cannot go back through bad works. The Greek language does indicate that we can backslide through doing the opposite of *pistis* (faith) which is expressed through the Greek word *apistos*. *Apistos* is the word for faithless. We get our word for apostasy from this word. The Scripture does indicate that you can cross back under the line but not through bad works, rather through a deliberate turning from God, or through denying your faith.

The apostle Peter gives a strong word about turning from your faith: "It would have been better for them not to have known the way of righteousness, than to have known it and then to turn their backs on the sacred command that was passed on to them" (2 Pet. 2:21). The prophet Ezekiel gives a similar warning: "But if a righteous man turns from his righteousness and commits sin and does the same detestable things the wicked man does, will he live? None of the righteous things he has done will be remembered. Because of the unfaithfulness he is guilty of and because of the sins he has committed, he will die" (Ezek. 18:24).

Holiness is on the top side of this imaginary line. We cannot become holy by abstaining from certain worldly things. Holiness means to be separate. When we cross this line through faith and submit our lives to Christ, we are made holy through Him. Holiness is Christ in us. However, because Christ is in us, we should then strive to live a life that glorifies Him, hence sanctification.

The soul that is devoted to seeking God refrains from worldliness because everything the devoted soul does is based on its love for God, not for self. The opposite of a soul devoted to seeking God is a soul devoted to seeking self-pleasure. Look at how Jesus refused worldliness because of His love for His father. In Matthew 4:8-10 we read, "Again, the devil took him to a very high mountain and showed him all the kingdoms of the world and their splendor. "All this I will give you," he said, "if you will bow down and worship me." Jesus said to him, "Away from me, Satan! For it is written: 'Worship the Lord your God, and serve him only.' "

Satan said, "I will give you the whole world and all its splendor if you would just bow down and worship me." To gain the world, you must worship Satan; to gain heaven you must worship God. The world and all its glory did not impress Jesus at all because He was devoted to His Father. If your heart and soul is not devoted to seeking God, He has no place to dwell within you.

## Devoted to God or Self?

If you are not devoted to God, then you are devoted to yourself. To be devoted to self leads you to worldliness, which could also be termed self-worship. If you become absorbed with the spirit of this world, you begin to put your life before others. You then begin to lose a true sense of the value of a soul. Whose soul is more valuable than Christ's? No one's! Yet Christ willingly gave up His soul for you and me. The only way He could give it up was to be more devoted to seeking His father than himself.

Consider Peter's words to us in 1 Peter 2:11: "Dear friends, I urge you, as aliens and strangers in the world, to abstain from sinful desires, which war against your soul." When something wars against your soul it is out to destroy your soul. However, the unique thing about destroying your soul is that it is done by challenging you to keep your soul for yourself. Sinful desires are designed to nurture your soul or flesh. They are lusts. They are things that so feed your soul that you no longer want to devote yourself to seeking God. Sinful desires are designed to get you to love your life or soul, rather than give it to God. This is what John 12:25 means: "The man who loves his life [soul] will lose it, while the man who hates his life [soul] in this world will keep it for eternal life."

### The Spirit of This World

First John 2:16 describes what we call the spirit of this world: "For everything in the world — the cravings of sinful man, the lust of his eyes and the boasting of what he has and does — comes not from the Father but from the world." Everything that is in the world falls under one of these three categories. The cravings of sinful man have to do with the lust of the flesh — sensual pleasures. The lust of the eyes has to do with materialism. It's being attracted to everything you can see with your eyes. The boasting of what a man has or does has to do with the pride of life. If your soul is captured by any one of these things, God has no dwelling place within you.

Consider Luke 14:16-24. "Jesus replied: 'A certain man was preparing a great banquet and invited many guests. At the time of the banquet he sent his servant to tell those who had been invited, "Come, for everything is now ready." But they all alike began to make excuses. The first said, "I have just bought a field, and I must go and see it. [Lust of the eyes, materialism.] Please excuse me." Another said, "I have just bought five yoke of oxen, and I'm on my way to try them out. [Boasting of what a man has or does, pride of life.] Please excuse me." Still another said, "I just got married, so I can't come." [Lust of the flesh.] The servant came back and reported this to his master. Then the owner of the house became angry'"

Look at what he says in verse 24: "Go out to the roads and country lanes and make them come in, so that my house will be full. I tell you, not one of those men who were invited will get a taste of my banquet."

When we get caught up in the spirit of this world, we will literally deny ourselves eternal life just so we can satisfy our flesh one more time. Consider Galatians 5:17. "For the sinful nature desires what is contrary to the Spirit, and the Spirit what is contrary to the sinful nature. They are in conflict with each other, so that you do not do what you want." The flesh and the spirit are in a constant struggle to keep us from doing the things we want to do. What we give ourselves to the most determines the outcome of our life. If we give ourselves over to the demands of the flesh more than the demands of the spirit, we will develop things in our lives that will keep us living within the spirit of this world.

The flesh and the spirit produce their own results. Look at Galatians 5:19-21. "The acts of the sinful nature are obvious: sexual immorality, impurity and debauchery; idolatry and witchcraft; hatred, discord, jealousy, fits of rage, selfish ambition, dissensions, factions and envy; drunkenness, orgies, and the like. I warn you, as I did before, that those who live like this will not inherit the kingdom of God."

All of these things are from living in the spirit of this world. However, God has something better for us. If we will live in His Spirit, the outcome of our life will be much different. "But the fruit of the Spirit is love, joy, peace, patience, kindness, goodness, faithfulness, gentleness and self-control. Against such things there is no law"

(Gal. 5:22-23). A life full of love, joy, and peace is a much better life than one filled with immorality, jealousy, and envy.

## The Devoted (Seeking) Soul

How do we develop a soul that seeks God? First of all we have to make a definite decision to serve God. Then comes the dying or burning. There must be a willful determination on your part to die to fleshly desires that would love to control you. However, the only way to stay committed to that type of thing is through a deep love for God.

We need a heart like King David's. In Psalm 42:1-2 we read, "As the deer pants for streams of water, so my soul pants for you, O God. My soul thirsts for God, for the living God. When can I go and meet with God?" To simply abstain from worldliness may not be anything more than legalism until we add a desire for God to it. If we are doing or not doing something because we do not want to do anything to hinder our pursuit of God, then we have pure motives, and we do not become legalists. There must be a passion for God so that we don't just become religious.

## A Heart to Know

Look at Jeremiah 24:7, "I will give them a heart to know me, that I am the Lord. They will be my people, and I will be their God, for they will return to me with all their heart." Ask God to give you a heart to know Him.

There is something about making God your pursuit that cleanses the soul. When I first started praying, I would pray for God to use me in the gifts. I was seeking the gifts. I wanted to flow in the gifts. However, it became a frustrating thing for me because all God would say to me was, "Just seek My Son." I thought I was. I would say, "God I want to flow in the gifts of the Spirit." All God would say back to me was, "Seek, My Son."

I thought being used by God and doing what I considered, "great things for God," had to come through the use of the gifts, and that, in essence, was seeking His Son. I thought being used was all God was interested in. After a while I began to realize that God wanted to work in me not just through me. God taught me some important lessons in the first few years of praying an hour a day. Seeking Him, pursuing Him, going after Him, and developing a seeking soul was what He wanted. That pursuit has become the greatest source of blessing and ministry in my life.

"When I was in distress, I sought the Lord; at night I stretched out untiring hands and my soul refused to be comforted" (Ps. 77:2). Have you ever stretched out untiring hands because your soul could not be satisfied with anything less than an answer from God? The stretched-out hand is the sign of surrender. If someone were to put a gun to your back, you would stretch out or lift your hands. The surrendered life is a devoted life. It is a life that has been given over to God and now His desires control you.

Years ago I would go to bed at 10:00 p.m., then I would rise at 3:00 a.m. and pray for two hours. Then at 5:00 a.m. I would go back to bed and sleep until 8:00 a.m. It was during this time in my life that I put myself on a trek toward knowing God.

I remember one night I had been praying for some time, and I was getting a little tired. I began to reason with God as to why I should go to bed a little early that night. One of my excuses was that I had been praying for a particular family in which I really didn't see anything happening. So I said to the Lord, "I think I will go to bed early tonight. After all I've only been praying for this family, and nothing is really happening there anyway."

When I said that, the Lord spoke back to me and said, "Ron, you are the only person praying for that family. Don't stop now."

It was as if God was saying, "Continue to stretch out untiring hands. Don't stop praying." Suddenly my soul refused to be comforted, and I continued to pray for them late into the morning.

Is your soul a seeking soul? Are you devoted to God? Is he consuming you? If not, you will never really be used by God to affect the souls of other men. There must be a passion for God. Your soul must cry out for the living God. Your soul must beat after God the way the deer pants after the water brook. Pray for God to give you a seeking soul. What if you are the only one who will pray for your family?

[1]Dr. Gordon Anderson, from a speech at the Wisconsin Family Camp for Wisconsin Assemblies of God, 1994.

# Chapter 11

# *Soul Winners*

A sold-out soul is a soul concerned for others. It is a soul that is consumed with the things that consume God. The men that have done "great things for God" are all men that had a passion for the lost.

When Henry Martyn was a boy in England he read a book on the life of David Brainerd. David Brainerd was a missionary to the American Indians. Brainerd's diary on prayer has influenced many of our great Christian leaders, including Jonathan Edwards and William Carey.

Brainerd's sold-out soul also convinced Henry Martyn to become the same. Martyn once said, "Let me burn-out for God." He did just that! Martyn died when he was 31 years old, however, before he died he translated the Bible into an Indian language and then translated it into the language of the Persians and Arabs. Whenever he went to the Middle East he presented the gospel to Moslems and Jews. Martyn's last trip was a 1,300-mile ride by horseback from Persia to Turkey. He may have burned-out; however, because he was sold-out, he accomplished more than most have accomplished in a lifetime.

### Every Living Soul

Every living soul belongs to God. The righteous soul and the wicked soul are both God's. Not all people call God their father. Not all people call Christ their Saviour. However, all people have been created by God, and their souls rightfully belong to God. Nevertheless, God has given us a free will. We have the ability to give our soul to God or to keep it for ourselves. In Ezekiel 18:4 we read, "For every living soul belongs to me, the father as well as the son — both alike belong to me. The soul who sins is the one who will die."

Because of God's love for all souls, it is impossible to draw close to God and not gain a burden for the lost. Church history shows that every true move of God has resulted in a missionary thrust. How a movement views the lost often determines how godly it is. Anything that God is involved in requires the death of self. Subsequently, it ultimately focuses more on others than it does itself. Missions and evangelism are the natural results of drawing close to God. When we get away from God, we lose a real sense of what God feels for the lost.

The closer you get to God, the more you feel what God feels about the souls of men. You cannot continue to draw close to God and refuse to deal with this issue. The more you take on the heart of God, the more your own heart beats as His. Every soul belongs to God and God deserves to gain every soul. As movements of God get away from prayer and drawing close to Him, they begin to downplay the need for missions and become more self-centered.

### Christ's Priestly Prayer

Consider Christ's priestly prayer in John 17:17-21, "Sanctify them by the truth; your word is truth. As you sent me into the world, I have sent them into the world.

For them I sanctify myself, that they too may be truly sanctified. My prayer is not for them alone. I pray also for those who will believe in me through their message, that all of them may be one, Father, just as you are in me and I am in you. May they also be in us so that the world may believe that you have sent me."

## Separation

Christ had a heart that beat after His Father's. In this prayer, He says many significant things. First, He talks about sanctification. "Sanctify them by the truth." Sanctification means to be set apart from the world. God's Word sets us apart. It's what we see in John 17:14, "I have given them your word and the world has hated them, for they are not of the world any more than I am of the world." Because the world hates the believer, there is a separation that takes place naturally just because we are Christians. However, sanctification involves two types of separation. There is a separation from the world, as indicated in 2 Timothy 2:21: "If a man cleanses himself from the latter, he will be an instrument for noble purposes, made holy, useful to the Master and prepared to do any good work." To cleanse ourselves is the same as separating ourselves. In this case, it is to separate ourselves from something.

There is also a separation unto God, as we see in Acts 26:18: "To open their eyes and turn them from darkness to light, and from the power of Satan to God, so that they may receive forgiveness of sins and a place among those who are sanctified by faith in me." We are to not only become separate from the world but we are to do that for *the purpose of separating ourselves unto God.* Separation from the world alone is not what draws people to Christ. We see this type of separation in the Amish and Mennonite type faiths. They practice a separation from the world. However, that separation alone is not enough for salvation. Our sins are not removed through abstaining from worldly activities. Rather, our sins are removed through separating ourselves unto Jesus and giving our lives to Him.

It's when we are separated unto God that people begin to see their need for Christ because that is when others begin to see Christ in us. Christ prayed that we would become one with him the same way he is one with the Father so that the world would believe.

Consider Hebrews 12:14: "Make every effort to live in peace with all men and to be holy; without holiness no one will see the Lord." The word "holy" here is the same word for sanctification. God wants us to live holy lives or sanctified lives. However, separation from the world alone is not enough. To live separate from the world might mean that we no longer take drugs, or that we no longer go to the same worldly places we used to go. But that alone is not what causes people to see Christ in us. It's when we are separated unto God that people really begin to see Jesus.

Hebrews instructs us to "Make every effort to live at peace with all men and to be holy; without holiness no one will see the Lord." I used to think that this verse meant we had to live holy lives so we could one day see Christ. There is truth in that statement. We must live holy so that one day we will see God. However, that would be a misapplication of this verse. This verse is not talking about us seeing the Lord at all. It's talking about our neighbors seeing Christ. In order for them to see Christ, we must be holy or separated unto God. To be separated from the world deals with our physical actions in life. To be separated unto God deals with our godly character. It's godly character that shows others their need for Christ.

If our neighbors do something evil to us and we do something kind in return, what will happen? They will begin to see that we do not live in the same world that they live in. They live in a world where it's an eye for an eye, and a tooth for a tooth. When they do something evil, they expect something evil in return. Therefore, if we return good for their evil, it separates us from their world. They see that there is something different about us. The verse then says in essence that without that separation or holiness, *they* (our neighbors) would never see the Lord. Lost souls see Christ because of our separation unto Him, not just because we separate ourselves from the world. So Christ prays in essence, "Sanctify them by your word, so that the world may see Me through them and believe."

Christ would do anything to glorify His Father. He proved that through His willingness to die. However, because of His deep love for His Father, He didn't even see His death as a terrible thing. Look at Isaiah 53:11, "After the suffering of his soul, he will see the light [of life] and be satisfied ; by his knowledge my righteous servant will justify many, and he will bear their iniquities." Christ looks back at the suffering of His own soul and is satisfied. Why? Because through His suffering, man now has available to him the redemption of his soul. Christ went through suffering, yet in retrospect it means very little in regard to its pain because of what it produced. Do you understand? God is interested in one thing: souls. He will pay any price for souls, He will do anything to win them. God will go to the ends of the earth to find a lost soul.

## *God of the Lost*

Consider just how far God will go to win a soul. In Genesis 16:1-8 we read,

> Now Sarai, Abram's wife, had borne
> him no children. But she had an Egyptian
> maidservant named Hagar; so she said to

Abram, "The Lord has kept me from having children. Go, sleep with my maidservant; perhaps I can build a family through her." Abram agreed to what Sarai said. So after Abram had been living in Canaan ten years, Sarai his wife took her Egyptian maidservant Hagar and gave her to her husband to be his wife. He slept with Hagar, and she conceived. When she knew she was pregnant, she began to despise her mistress. Then Sarai said to Abram, "You are responsible for the wrong I am suffering. I put my servant in your arms, and now that she knows she is pregnant, she despises me. May the Lord judge between you and me." "Your servant is in your hands," Abram said. "Do with her whatever you think best." Then Sarai mistreated Hagar; so she fled from her. The angel of the Lord found Hagar near a spring in the desert; it was the spring that is beside the road to Shur. And he said, "Hagar, servant of Sarai, where have you come from, and where are you going?" "I'm running away from my mistress Sarai," she answered.

Sarai had become so envious of her maid that she mistreated her to the point that Hagar fled from her presence. She stopped at a spring in the desert and the angel of the Lord found her there by the water. Look at what the angel tells her to do in verse 9: "Then the angel of the Lord told her, "Go back to your mistress and submit to her."

Hagar was pregnant. A seed had been planted within her and now she was running from that whole situation. It is not very different from how many of us came to the

Lord. At some point, the seed of the gospel was planted within us. Maybe it came through someone witnessing to us. Maybe it came through attending church as a child. Maybe it was through something we read. Regardless of how it came, it impregnated us with the gospel. Then we came face to face with whether or not we would submit to it.

Initially the gospel seems too hard to follow. It seems we could never live the way Christ wants us to live. Because of that many start a life of running from God. We may not even consider it running from God, but God has His seed in us, and our rebellion is seen by Him as running from Him.

The truly important thing for us to grasp here is how God came to Hagar in the middle of the desert. Here you have God revealing himself to the utterly poor, the afflicted one. By the time Hagar had gotten to the spring in the desert she was without hope and confused. But that is where God met her. Hagar names the spring *Beer-Lahai-roi*. That name carries within it this meaning; *the God that lives and sees me.* Look at Genesis 16:13, "She gave this name to the Lord who spoke to her: 'You are the God who sees me,' for she said, 'I have now seen the One who sees me.'" This is the wonder of the ages. When God comes to those who have absolutely no hope, no direction, no means of helping themselves, it is more than we can comprehend. Why would God in heaven be concerned about the hopeless? It's because He is love.

## The One Who Sees and Hears

Why does it seem that this God of love allows us to come to a point of hopelessness? I believe it's primarily the fact that *when we have no hope, we are ready to submit.* Do you remember what God told Hagar in verse 9? "Go back and submit." When we have been stripped of all hope, we are finally ready to bring our lives under the control of someone else. Submission means to bring yourself under. Now look at verse 10, "The angel added, 'I will so increase your descendants that they will be too numerous to count.' " Once we submit our lives to God, we become the bride of Christ. The Bride is the only one who gives birth. Christ cannot give birth. It is the exclusive function of the Bride. This is why He calls us to submission. Submission is intimacy. It's only through intimacy that you give birth. There is no giving birth without intimacy. If we will submit to God, we will give birth to more than we can count. Our submission to God will result in people being born into God's kingdom.

Hagar, the utterly poor and afflicted one, learned one of the greatest secrets in the history of God's Word. God taught her that He SEES and hears the cry of the afflicted. It is not a small thing when God reveals himself. And He has done so, in most cases, as a direct result of the cry of the afflicted.

Hagar does what God asks her to do, and she returns to Sarai to submit to her. Later on, she is again driven out from Abram's home. This is very typical. When we first are saved, we are called to submit to God. Through that submission, we are brought into His family. Within His family there is warmth and comfort. There is nurturing and there is spiritual food. In fact there is so much food that we begin to grow spiritually. With growth and maturity, it is not uncommon for God to ask us to leave the comfort zone. Many times He calls us back to the desert for another time of learning. Sometimes the desert comes in the form of some type of ministry.

There are countless numbers of those who, in answer to God's call, have found themselves in the desert. There is really nothing simple about following God. However, that is not what's important. The important thing is that regardless of where we are with God, He is big enough to help us.

So once again Hagar is found wandering through the desert, but this time she is with her son. After all her water is gone, all her hope is gone, and her son is dying, the angel of God reveals himself to her. He repeats His promise to her that He would make of the child a great nation, and He opened her eyes and showed her a well of water. Hagar then disappears from any more mention in the Scriptures. Ishmael grew and became a nation.

Men often try to build kingdoms unto themselves, when in reality God is simply calling them to serve Him. It is not uncommon for a man to accomplish the very thing God has called them to, and then they disappear from view. Then those they gave birth to take over. This is what John the Baptist experienced. He was not called to build anything around him. He was called to make a straight path through the wilderness and to call men to repentance. Once he had accomplished that, he disappeared from view and the Lamb of God, the very one he baptized, takes over.

What do you think God is hearing and seeing today? The God who hears the cry of the afflicted is hearing and seeing the afflicted. Even in the uttermost parts of the earth, He hears and sees. And He calls to us to be the one who will bring the message of hope to them. How many of us can relate to Hagar's experience? How many of us were hopeless and afflicted when God heard our cry and came to us?

### Utilitarians?

It will be important at this point for us to understand what utilitarian Christianity is. It is a Christianity that makes God a means rather than the glorious end that He is. It's a type of Christianity where you use God to get all the things you ever wanted. It's giving your life to

Christ strictly for the purpose of going to heaven one day without any regard for the lost souls around you. It is a self-centered Christianity. It is also a type of Christianity that cannot see beyond self and therefore will never focus on missions or on others.

God heard our cry when we had nothing to offer Him. We were utterly poor and afflicted, we had nothing to donate back to God, with one exception — our soul. When we gave our life to Christ, we gave Him our soul. In exchange, He gave us His life. We are now owned by Him. We are not to use God to get all the things we ever wanted. Christianity is not about God glorifying us. It's about us glorifying Christ. We are to serve God for one reason. He is worthy! We are to serve God even if it meant in the end we would go to hell, because He is worthy of our service. This life is not about what we are going to get out of God. This life is about what God is going to get out of us.

Paul has a different type of Christianity in mind than utilitarian Christianity when he stated in Philippians 2:5-8, "Your attitude should be the same as that of Christ Jesus: Who, being in very nature God, did not consider equality with God something to be grasped, [Utilitarian Christianity considers equality with God as something to be grasped, therefore it reaches for all it can get], but made himself nothing, taking the very nature of a servant, being made in human likeness. And being found in appearance as a man, He humbled himself and became obedient to death — even death on a cross!"

### Two Moravians

Paris Reidhead in his message, "Ten Shekels for a Shirt," once told a true story about how two young Moravian men heard of an island in the West Indies where an atheist British owner had two to three thousand slaves. The owner had said no preacher or clergymen would ever stay on this island. If a preacher was shipwrecked on his island, the owner vowed to keep him in a separate house until he could leave, but then he would never be permitted to talk to anyone about Christ. Three thousand slaves from the jungles of Africa were brought to this island in the Atlantic Ocean. There they would live and die without hearing of Christ.

These two young Moravians heard about this and decided that the only way they could get the message to these who were lost was to become slaves themselves. So they sold themselves to the British planter and used the money they received to pay their passage for a one-way boat fare. They had no plans of ever seeing their home again, for they sold themselves into lifetime slavery. It was the only way they could get the gospel to those who were crying and afflicted.

As the ship left the port their families who came to see them off were there weeping because they knew they would never see them again. They wondered why they were going. They questioned the wisdom of what they were doing. As the ship made its way away from the shore one of the young boys (they were only in their twenties), could be heard in the distance shouting, "May the Lamb that was slain, receive the reward of his suffering," never to be heard from again.

This saying became the call of Moravian missions. The Moravians went on to become the first really organized modern day missions thrust. *May the Lamb that was slain receive the reward of his suffering.* The reward of his suffering is the salvation of our souls. Jesus did not consider equality with God something to be grasped, but made himself nothing, taking the very nature of a servant. *This is the only reason for being, that Christ would receive the reward of his suffering.* Let that mind be in you.

# Chapter 12

# *Who Will You Be in Glory?*

What is the first thing that comes to your mind at the mention of the apostle Peter's name? What is the first thing you think of when you hear the name General MacArthur? What comes to your mind at the mention of Hitler? Rarely do we think of the physical stature of a man at the mention of his name. At the mention of General MacArthur's name you probably thought of a soldier or the man who dropped the bomb on Japan. At the mention of Peter's name you may have thought of a fisherman or an Apostle. Names tend to describe what a person is known for more so than what they look like. If I said, Billy Graham, you probably would not think, a tall man with grey hair. You would think: Evangelist!

At the mention of the name Johann Sebastian Bach you think musician. The Bach's lived in Germany for more than two centuries as a family of musicians. In that particular region of the country, if an exceptional musician was heard, the people would say, "He is a real 'Bach' for sure." It went so far that they even used the name

"Bach" when they meant musician. Proverbs 22:1 says, "A good name is more desirable than great riches." A man's name does more than just tag some type of identification mark on him. It really describes a certain quality about him.

It is one thing to have a good name here on earth, however, something that will prove to be even more important than a good name on earth is who you will be in glory. The Bible indicates that God has a new name or identity for each of us. Consider the following verses regarding a new name: "The nations will see your righteousness, and all kings your glory; you will be called by a new *name* that the mouth of the Lord will bestow" (Isa. 62:2). "He who has an ear, let him hear what the Spirit says to the churches. To him who overcomes, I will give some of the hidden manna. I will also give him a white stone with a *new name* written on it, known only to him who receives it" (Rev. 2:17). "Him who overcomes I will make a pillar in the temple of my God. Never again will he leave it. I will write on him the name of my God and the name of the city of my God, the new Jerusalem, which is coming down out of heaven from my God; and I will also write on him my *new name*" (Rev. 3:12).

The new name is usually connected with the overcomer. A God-given name has to do with who you really are. We humans seem to simply tag names on things without giving a lot of thought to their meanings. We give names like Bob, or Ted, or Bill. God appears to take names more seriously than we do. It seems that from God's perspective, names are actually a description of a person's character. Names like "Faithful," "Steadfast," "Warrior," "Shepherd," and "Joyful" are found throughout the Scriptures.

## Overcoming

There is an overcoming that goes before the endowment of any godly characteristic upon a person. In the overcoming process, we develop the character that describes our new name. What does it mean to be an overcomer? Basically it means that we must overcome the world. But what is the world? Is it Hollywood? Is it rock and roll music? Is it alcohol and drugs? To all of these the answer is "No." What is the world then? It is nothing more than the worship of man. Humanism is the essence of worldliness, and it manifests itself through things that glorify man, like Hollywood, rock and roll, and so forth. Man glorifying man, rather than God, is the struggle we are all involved in. Through the death of self-glorification, all these other activities will fall away.

In 1 John 2:15-16 we read, "Do not love the world or anything in the world. If anyone loves the world, the love of the Father is not in him. For everything in the world — the cravings of sinful man, the lust of his eyes and the boasting of what he has and does — comes not from the Father but from the world."

The spirit of this world all centers around man. It is comprised of three things. First, there is the lust of the flesh. This deals with sensuality. Man has a great natural desire to satisfy his flesh. Second, there is the lust of the eyes. This deals with materialism. It is an attraction to the things you can see with your eye. Third, there is the pride of life. This is the boasting of the things you have and can accomplish on your own. Each one of these three issues focus on man rather than on God. Overcoming the world then is gaining victory in each of these areas.

### The White Stone

Overcoming is a process. It is not something we accomplish by simply deciding to be an overcomer. While a person is in the process of overcoming, he develops within himself the very qualities of God that his God-given name proclaims. God is going to give a trophy with a new name written upon it to the ones who overcome. "I will also give him a white stone with a new name written on it, known only to him who receives it" (Rev. 2:17).

The white stone mentioned in this verse is similar to what we would call a trophy. In Bible days, if a person had won some type of contest he would receive a white stone, just as a modern athlete is awarded a trophy. The stone would have some type of inscription on it describing something unique about the one receiving it. The same is true today. If you received a trophy for winning a marathon, the inscription on it would describe something unique to you.

I once had an opportunity to conduct a prayer seminar in Hawaii. I happened to be there at the same time of the Ironman Triathalon. From my motel room I could see both the starting point and the finish line. At 6:00 a.m. 1,500 men and women dove into the ocean to swim 2.2 miles. After the swim they would jump on bicycles and peddle for 110 miles. When they finished with that they would then run a 26-mile marathon. The man who won finished the race right at the eight-hour mark. For over eight hours he pushed his body beyond its natural limits. He was awarded a large trophy with his name inscribed on it.

Why was the trophy given to him? Because he won! Why did he win? Because he possessed the qualities described on the trophy. How is it he possessed those qualities? Through training and character development. The same is true of us spiritually. In the process of becoming an overcomer, we develop the very qualities of the name God gives us.

## A New Name

Revelation 2:17 says that the name on the white stone is only known to the one who receives it. Think of the intimacy of that. What this tells us is that there is a very special relationship between the overcomer and God. The name on the white stone is very similar to what we call a "nick-name." However, this is more than just a cute little name that God has attached to each of us. This name describes a certain quality of God himself. But why should this be a secret? Why not let the whole world know this name? Because this name describes a God-like quality we possess. What would happen to the average man if God were to announce to the whole world how that man reflects Him? Pride would ruin his life. Pride is what the spirit of this world is all about.

What would the average man take the most pride in? God-likeness! We love to have people refer to ourselves in a way that identifies us with our heavenly father. God-likeness signifies God's approval of us. When someone approaches us and says something like, "You are so faithful in the things of God," it makes us feel good because of how that identifies us with our heavenly Father. It's human nature to love being identified with someone we respect or revere.

Once when my son was about 10 years old we were on our way to visit his grandparents for Christmas. We had traveled for many hours and had many more to go when we decided to take a break by stopping at a Christian bookstore that was on the way. My wife wandered off by herself and my son and I were in an aisle looking for one of my books. I didn't see what I was looking for so I went to the counter to ask a clerk if he had my newest book (I did not tell him I was the author).

The clerk looked it up and said, "We are out of it, but we have it on order. It's by a man named Ron Auch."

I said, "Thanks," and walked off. My son asked me why I didn't tell him that I was Ron Auch. I just told him I didn't think I needed to. I could tell that my son was bothered by this.

Later it was time to go and my son and I were standing in the middle of an aisle very close to the clerk who had helped us earlier. I told my son it was time to go and I started to walk away. I noticed that my son was not following me so I raised my voice a little and said, "We have to get going."

My son looked at me and then looked at the clerk and in a very loud voice said, "WHY WOULD RON AUCH WANT TO LEAVE THE BOOK STORE SO SOON?" He was determined to let that man know who I was. *I now take my son to every bookstore I ever go to.* We like to be identified with those we respect and love.

What was it Satan wanted Jesus to do in the wilderness temptation? He wanted Jesus to simply bow down and worship him. "All this I will give you," he said, "if you will bow down and worship me" (Matt. 4:9). What could be more fulfilling to the carnal mind than that very thing? Consider how some evangelists boast of what God does in their services. It is not uncommon to see boasts on their posters like, "GREATEST MIRACLES THIS SIDE OF HEAVEN," or "THOUSANDS OF PEOPLE SAVED IN EACH SERVICE!" Rarely do we see what we likely should see on their posters. We should probably see things that refer to the evangelist himself like, "Chastised by God!" "Under Judgment!" or "Needs to Repent!" Preachers love to be called anointed. Our love to be called "anointed" is proof that we aren't as anointed as we think we are.

What would happen if God were to make a public statement about us the way He did His Son? "And a voice from heaven said, 'This is my Son, whom I love; with him I am well pleased' " (Matt. 3:17). If this happened to the average man, the pride of his life would ruin any ministry he had. However, there is a difference between the average man and the overcomer. The overcomer has successfully gained victory in the battle over self-glory.

## Who We Really Are

The name God gives us is who we really are. It's the very qualities of God that we possess, but it's not for us to boast about. It's for us to take into our heart and cherish there. We are not to stand in the public eye and tell others how faithful we are or how virtuous we are. These qualities are literally the essence of our relationship with God.

The question must still be asked, "Who will we be in glory?" The be-ing, or who we will be, will be determined by the overcoming. It will take God-like qualities in order to be victorious in the battle to overcome. This is how the one who is overcoming is continually developing in his God-likeness.

This whole issue deals with eternity and how God is preparing us for the life to come. Who will we be in glory? There is a life to come that we sometimes forget about and even more rarely prepare for. Our tendency is to forget about eternity while we are in the midst of overcoming. Overcoming signifies a battle. In the midst of the fray, we often forget that there is more to life than the current life we are in. The battles we go through today have much more to do with eternity than we realize.

## Bible Days

Consider the day we live in. We live in Bible days, the same way those we read of in the Bible did. These are the days of the fulfillment of the Book of Revelation. These are the last days. Often we read about certain Bible characters and envy them. We think it would have been wonderful to have lived in those days. Someday in the future, people will look at us and say, "You were one of those who lived during the last days. What was it like to live in Bible times?" Is it possible you, too, could be someone whom the people in the future read about concerning some spiritual event?

Consider both Moses and Elijah. They both went through many battles while they were on earth. Do you think they had any idea that one day they would be characters in the Bible and examples that God uses to show others how to live? Not everything in Moses' life was easy. At one time Moses had to run for his life. "When Pharaoh heard of this, he tried to kill Moses, but Moses fled from Pharaoh and went to live in Midian, where he sat down by a well" (Exod. 2:15). While Moses was running for his life, do you believe he even considered himself a spiritual man?

Then while Moses was leading the people of God through the desert, he ran into many more problems. "So the people grumbled against Moses, saying, 'What are we to drink?' " (Exod. 15:24). When people grumble against you, it tends to make you feel a little insecure.

Then God called Moses to the top of the mountain to give him the Ten Commandments. Certainly this would restore his sense of spiritual leadership. However, as he came back down the mountain he was shaken into reality. "When Moses approached the camp and saw the calf and the dancing, his anger burned and he threw the tablets, breaking them to pieces at the foot of the mountain" (Exod. 32:19). After an experience like that, Moses probably wondered if there was any hope at all.

Elijah was no stranger to highs and lows either. "Elijah went before the people and said, 'How long will you waver between two opinions? If the Lord is God, follow him; but if Baal is God, follow him.' But the people said nothing" (1 Kings 18:21). Elijah challenges all the prophets of Baal. They accept the challenge but cannot produce. They fail in their attempt to prove that Baal is God. Elijah then prays to God and fire from heaven falls. "Then the fire of the Lord fell and burned up the sacrifice" (1 Kings 18:38). After Elijah demonstrated that his God was the one true God, he had all of Baal's prophets destroyed. This was one of the great highlights of his ministry. However, not long after that victory he was running for his life. "Elijah was afraid and ran for his life. When he came to Beersheba in Judah, he left his servant there" (1 Kings 19:3).

## *Mount of Transfiguration*

"After six days, Jesus took with him Peter, James and John the brother of James, and led them up a high mountain by themselves. There he was transfigured before them. His face shone like the sun, and his clothes became as white as the light. Just then there appeared before them Moses and Elijah, talking with Jesus" (Matt. 17:1-3).

Do you think Moses and Elijah had any idea that one day, hundreds of years after their deaths, they would appear with the very Son of God on the Mount of Transfiguration? When Moses and Elijah were going through their different struggles, do you think they had any idea they were being groomed for their life to come?

When David was being pursued through the wilderness by a king who wanted to take his life, do you think he had any idea that one day God would say of David, "The Lord has sought out a man after his own heart and appointed him leader of his people" (1 Sam. 13:14). After David had committed adultery with Bathsheba do you think he could have ever imagined himself as the one after whom they would name the City of David?

Do you believe Rahab the prostitute had any idea that Jesus would be her offspring, or that she would be in the lineage of the Messiah? When she was deep in sin, do you think she ever could have imagined herself as one of the people we would read about throughout eternity?

Do you think Isaiah had any idea that one day Jesus

would stand in the synagogue and quote his writings, proclaiming, "'The Spirit of the Lord is on me, because he has anointed me to preach good news to the poor. He has sent me to proclaim freedom for the prisoners and recovery of sight for the blind, to release the oppressed'" (Luke 4:18). Could you imagine what it would do to any of us today if Jesus ever quoted anything we said? That's why there must first be an overcoming of the pride of this life before anything like that could ever happen.

Do you think Daniel had any idea while he was standing in a lion's den that one day he would be given a vision that would be a primary source of our understanding of the end times? Do you think he thought that possibly this vision would be talked about thousands of years after he received it? These individuals were all overcomers. While they walked this earth they developed certain Godly attributes and characteristics. They now all have new names that reflect those qualities.

### The Prayer Life

I know of no better way to overcome the world than through the practice of prayer. Prayer is overcoming. Interestingly enough, overcoming is actually bringing yourself under God. Worldliness is exalting yourself. Prayer is humbling yourself.

Prayer puts the pray-er in the presence of God. It develops a hunger for God within you. It creates a desire for God that overcomes your desire for this world and all of its vain glory. While a person is in prayer they begin the process of developing the very qualities of God that will eventually become their ministry to others. Will you be one of His faithful ones? Will you be one of His loving ones? Will you be one of His joyful ones? Will you be one of His caring ones? Who will you be in glory? In the future, when your children hear your name, what will be the first thing they think of?

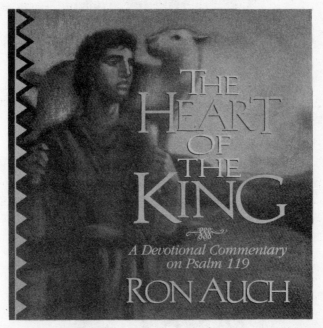

**Other books by Ron Auch:**

**The Seven Spirits of God** • The seven Spirits of God are mentioned four times in the Book of Revelation. What are they and how do they pertain to us?

The seven Spirits of God detail the biblical meaning of being "Spirit filled." God has a definite purpose in wanting His spirit to dwell within men. Peter defined it when he said, "You may participate in the (His) divine nature and escape the corruption in the world." The Spirit of God is to help us overcome the impurity of this world. This book challenges its readers to examine themselves to see if they emulate all of the fullness of God and are truly living the overcomer's life.    $8.95

*Available at bookstores nationwide or contact*
*New Leaf Press • P.O. Box 726 • Green Forest, AR 72638*